STANLEY SPENCER
and the English Garden

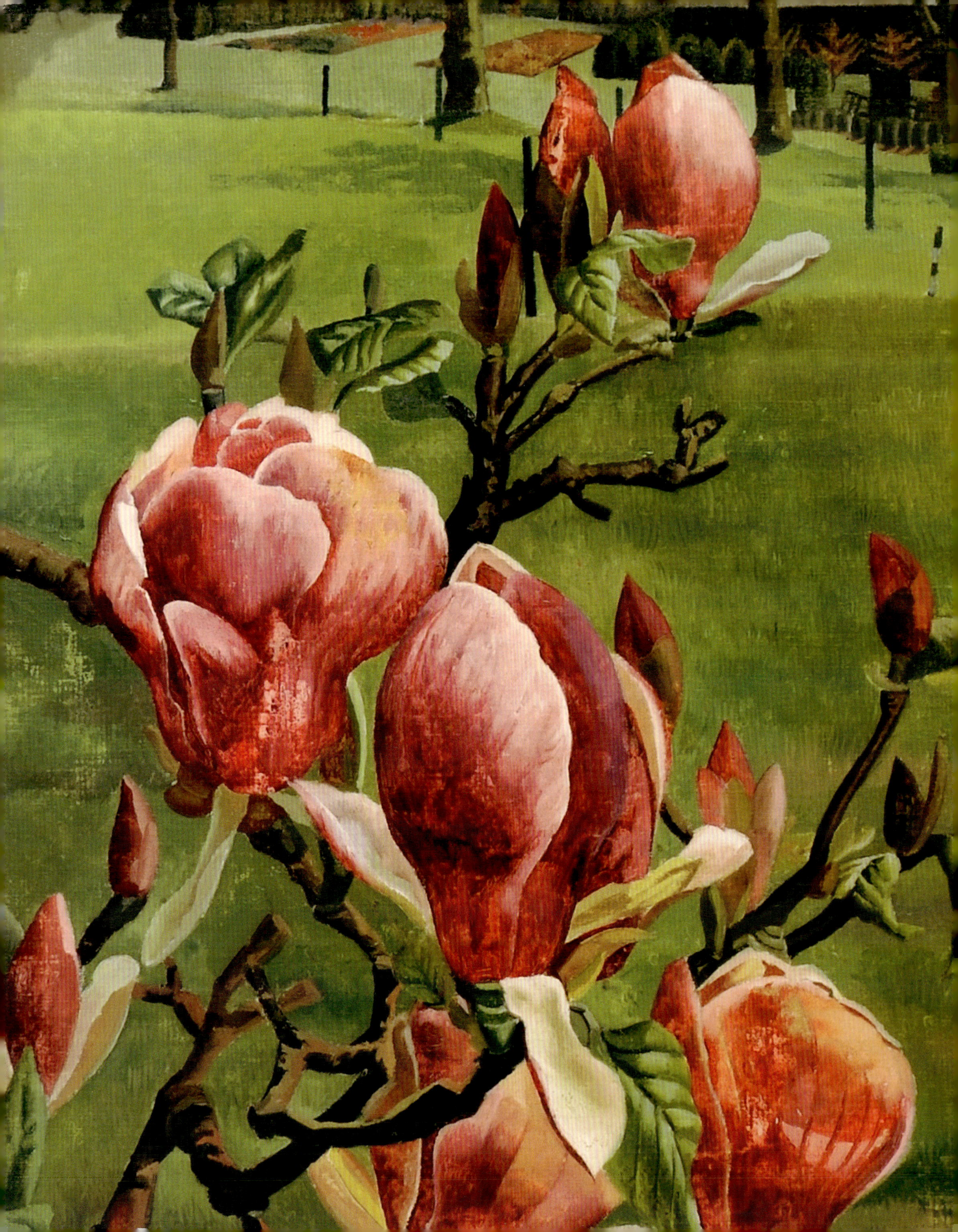

STANLEY SPENCER
and the English Garden

EDITED BY
Steven Parissien

Compton Verney
in association with
Paul Holberton publishing

EDITOR'S ACKNOWLEDGEMENTS

I am extremely grateful to all of our illustrious contributors for their excellent essays. Particular thanks are due to Dr Martin Postle – who provided both the original idea for this book and who co-curated the accompanying exhibition, which was shown at Compton Verney over the summer of 2011 – and Jenine McGaughran for the picture research.

I would like to extend my thanks to all those galleries and individuals who so kindly lent works to the exhibition, and who have given permission to illustrate their paintings in this book. Thanks are also due to Paul Holberton and his colleagues for their help, patience and expertise.

Lastly, a huge thank you to the Paul Mellon Centre for Studies in British Art, whose publication grant made the production of this book possible, and to the Peter Moores Foundation, whose financial support enabled us to stage the original 2011 exhibition.

CONTRIBUTORS

PROFESSOR KEITH BELL is Professor of Art History at the University of Saskatchewan.

PROFESSOR JEREMY GOULD is Emeritus Professor of Architecture at the University of Plymouth.

DR STEVEN PARISSIEN is Director of Compton Verney, Warwickshire.

DR MARTIN POSTLE is Assistant Director for Academic Activities at the Paul Mellon Centre for Studies in British Art, London.

PROFESSOR DUNCAN ROBINSON is Master of Magdalene College, Cambridge, and former Director of the Fitzwilliam Museum, Cambridge.

CONTENTS

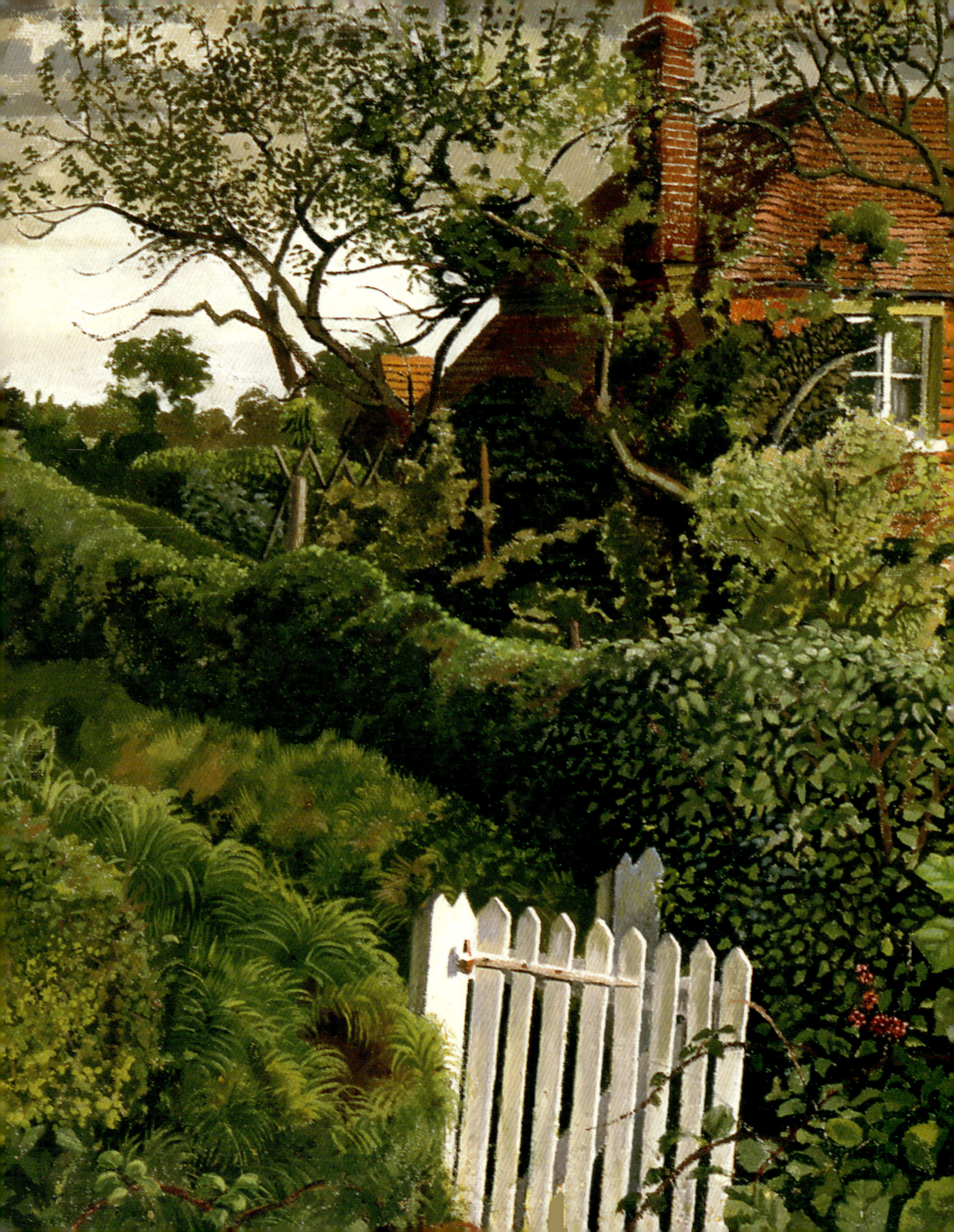

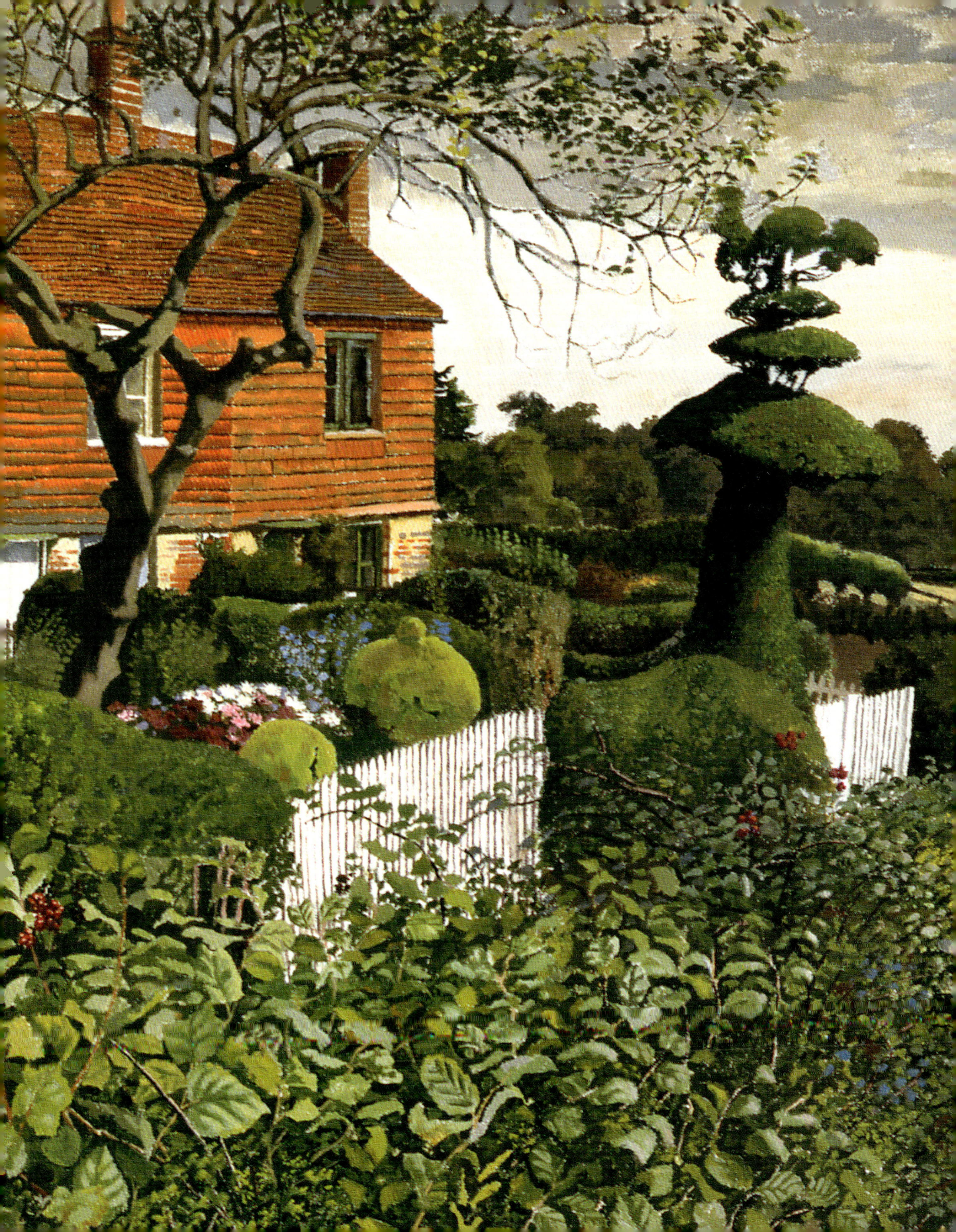

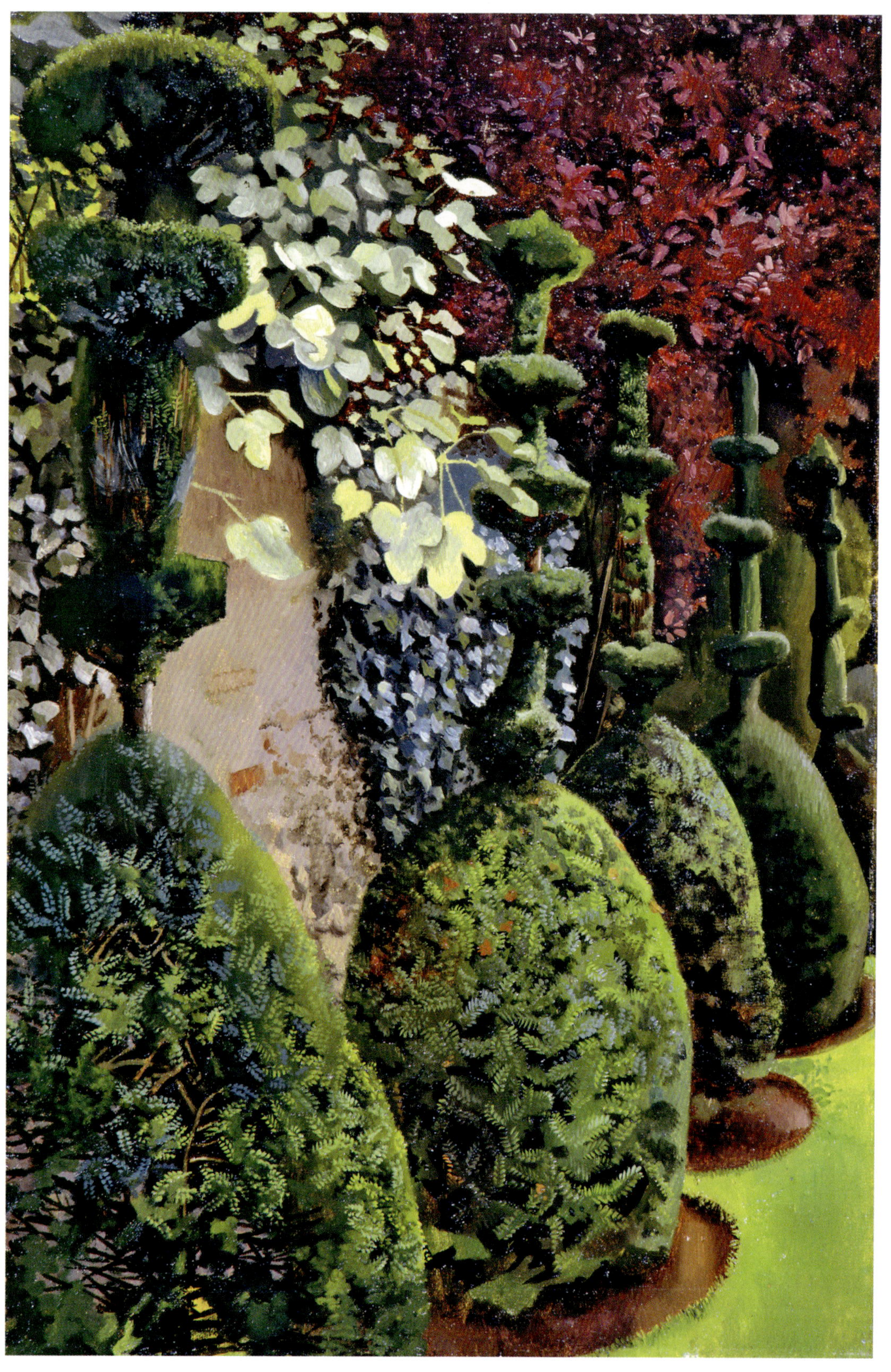

STANLEY SPENCER IN RETROSPECT

Duncan Robinson

In 1956, in the second volume of his *Modern English Painters*, John Rothenstein neatly summarized the problem of Spencer's reputation. "When *The Resurrection: Port Glasgow* [1947–50, Tate] was exhibited in 1950," he wrote, "the artists whose work I most admired and whose opinions I generally respected were among its severest critics." He went on to cite, at the more popular end of the critical spectrum, the verdict of Winston Churchill: "If that is the Resurrection, then give me eternal sleep." Spencer, it seemed, pleased neither the modernists nor the traditionalists.

As the Director of the Tate Gallery, Rothenstein had done his best to redress the balance in Spencer's favour by giving him a retrospective exhibition there in 1955. In the course of it Spencer was filmed for television. Looking back at that footage is to be reminded that he was one of the very first artists to conquer the medium, but he did so as a character, as the amiable eccentric who was to be remembered fondly by the residents of Cookham as they had seen him, pushing his painting cart, an old perambulator, down the street from his home in Cliveden View to his favourite spot among the gravestones in Holy Trinity churchyard. It was an image he did nothing to dispel during the last years of his life when he became, in the words of his brother Gilbert, "something of a public figure", and honours accrued, including the knighthood conferred on him shortly before he died. On the other hand, any well-disposed commentator who wished to champion Spencer the artist found it expedient to detach him from the artistic mainstream and to stress his individuality as a visionary artist, more akin to William Blake than to any of his contemporaries. Today Spencer is celebrated as a modern master, thanks to a seismic shift in taste. Twenty years after his death, he was revered by a generation of art students for whom he became, in the words of Lawrence Gowing, a kind of Old Testament prophet who paved the way for the restoration of faith in figurative painting. But it is important to remember that as far as he was concerned, as Eric Newton wrote in 1947, "each picture is a statement of a particular message, an illustration of a specific idea in pictorial form".

Stanley Spencer was born in the village of Cookham, Berkshire, on 30 June 1891, the tenth surviving child of William Spencer, 'Professor of Music, Organist of St Nicholas, Hedsor', according to the brass plate which was attached to the gate outside Fernlea, the family's home in Cookham High Street. He and Gilbert, the youngest of his siblings, were taught by their older sister Annie, who had taken over the schoolroom which their father had set up in an outbuilding at the bottom of the next-door garden. For the two small boys, so physically confined, "there were", as Gilbert recalled, "hidden bits of Cookham as remote as the Milky

1
STANLEY SPENCER
Clipped Yews, 1935
Oil on canvas, 76.2 x 50.8 cm
Aberdeen Art Gallery

Way". On the other hand their imaginative horizons were extended by their father's practice of music and his passion for literature. From W.T. Stearn's *Books for Bairns*, read to them by Annie, they graduated, via *Gulliver's Travels* and *Pilgrim's Progress*, to Shakespeare, Milton and the Bible, from which Spencer senior was particularly inclined to read aloud.

Unlike their predominantly musical siblings, Stanley and Gilbert Spencer displayed a talent for art. They got to know a local artist, William Bailey, whose daughter Dorothy gave them their first drawing lessons. Then, at sixteen, Stanley enrolled in classes at the Technical Institute in Maidenhead, just three miles from Cookham. From there he went, in 1908, to the Slade School of Fine Art in London, thanks to the intervention of one of his father's patrons and a former Slade student, Lady Boston, who offered to pay his fees if he were accepted. Spencer's four years at the Slade were definitive in terms of his artistic development. The early influence of the Pre-Raphaelites, and of book illustrations by Millais and Rackham, was broadened by exposure to a much wider spectrum of European art, including the graphic work of Dürer and Cranach in the Print Rooms of the Slade and the British Museum, and the paintings in the National Gallery, especially the early Italian schools. At the same time Spencer found himself in a talented peer group which included David Bomberg, Mark Gertler, Paul Nash, C.R.W. Nevinson and Edward Wadsworth. They and their contemporaries were not slow to react when, in 1910, Roger Fry launched the first of his exhibitions of recent French art, *Manet and the Post-Impressionists*, which opened at the Grafton Galleries that winter. Spencer's painting of *The Nativity* (1912, Slade School of Fine Art), for which he was awarded the Nettleship Prize in 1912, summarizes all of these influences: the composition, with the Madonna of Humility, makes an indirect reference to Piero della Francesca's unfinished painting of the same subject in the National Gallery; the impassive, mask-like faces of the bystanders have a passing resemblance to Gauguin's figures; the botanical accuracy of the flowering chestnut tree acknowledges an enduring respect for the Pre-Raphaelites.

Among the friends Spencer made at the Slade were Jacques Raverat and his future wife Gwen Darwin. The couple fuelled his interest in literature with gifts of books, including Ruskin's essay on *Giotto and his Works at Padua* and John Donne's *Sermons*. It was this last which gave rise to Spencer's painting of *John Donne arriving in Heaven* (1911, private collection), which Clive Bell chose to include in the second of Fry's Post-Impressionist exhibitions at the Grafton Galleries in 1912–13. The painting remains unusual in Spencer's oeuvre, derived perhaps as much from his reading of Ruskin's descriptions of Giotto's frescoes containing a "plain, masculine kind of people" as from his encounters with Post-Impressionism. What is certain is that in Spencer's mind there was one obvious location for heaven, "in this case a part of Widbrook Common".

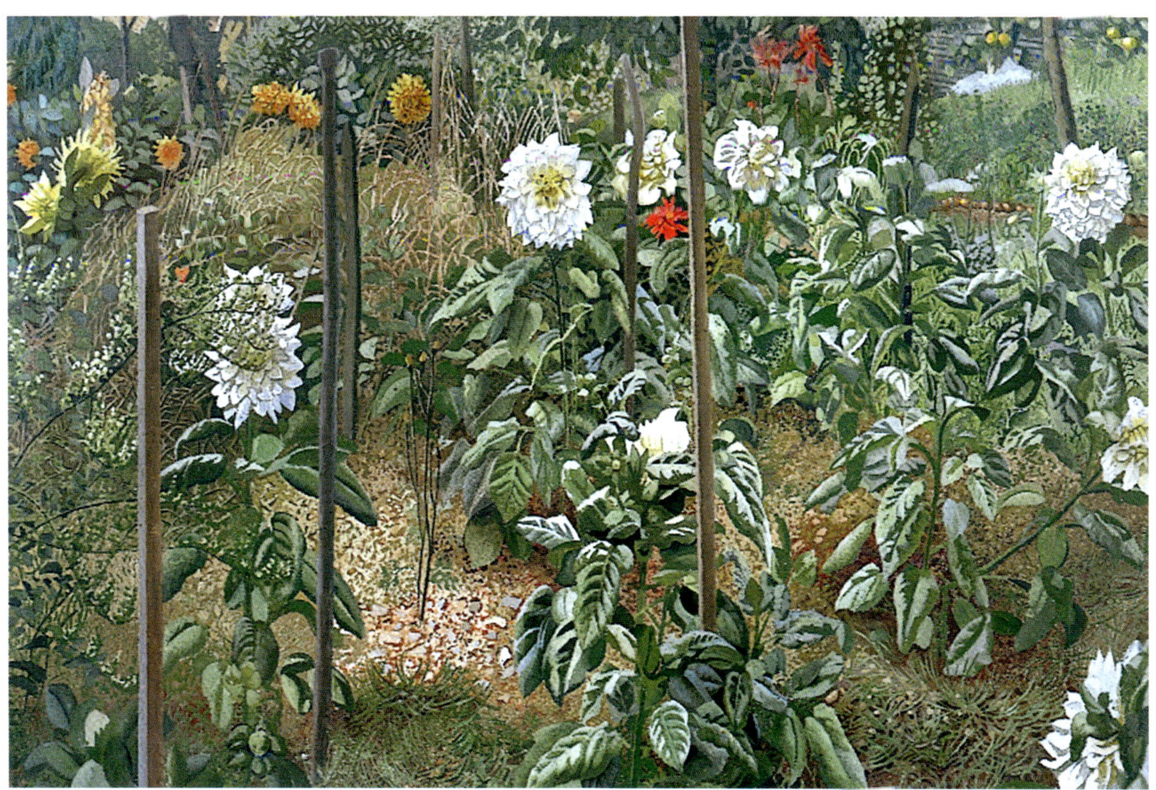

2
STANLEY SPENCER
Garden, Cookham Rise, 1946
Oil on canvas, 50.8 × 76.2 cm
Huddersfield Art Gallery

At the Slade, Spencer earned the nickname 'Cookham', partly because he continued to live there, commuting by train to London, but presumably also because his fellow-students knew that whatever subject he painted, he transferred it in his imagination to his own, familiar territory. His *Apple Gatherers* (1912–13, Tate) are placed in an orchard just beyond the garden of Fernlea; *The Visitation* (1912–13, Hunterian Museum and Art Gallery, Glasgow) features Dot Wooster, the butcher's daughter, and Peggy Hatch, a cousin, standing in the doorway of the old schoolroom next door; and *Zacharias and Elizabeth* (1914, Tate) are reunited in a garden Spencer could see from the landing window on the second floor of Wisteria Cottage. He was later to describe it as "an attempt to raise that life round me to what I felt was its true status, meaning and purpose. A version of the St Luke passage, the gardener dragging the branch of ivy, and Mrs Gooden giving me permission to walk about the garden ... the whole of what I hoped was dependent on the reality of everyday life."

In Cookham he had found his "earthly paradise", only to lose it almost immediately "when along comes the war and smashes everything". In July 1915, Spencer enlisted in the Royal Army Medical Corps and, after spending nine months as an orderly at the Beaufort War Hospital, he signed up for overseas service. He served at first with the 68th Field Ambulances in Macedonia before volunteering, in August 1917, to join a fighting unit, the 7th Battalion of the Royal Berkshire Regiment. News reached him of his appointment as an official war artist, but it was a bout of malaria which finally invalided him out of the front line. By

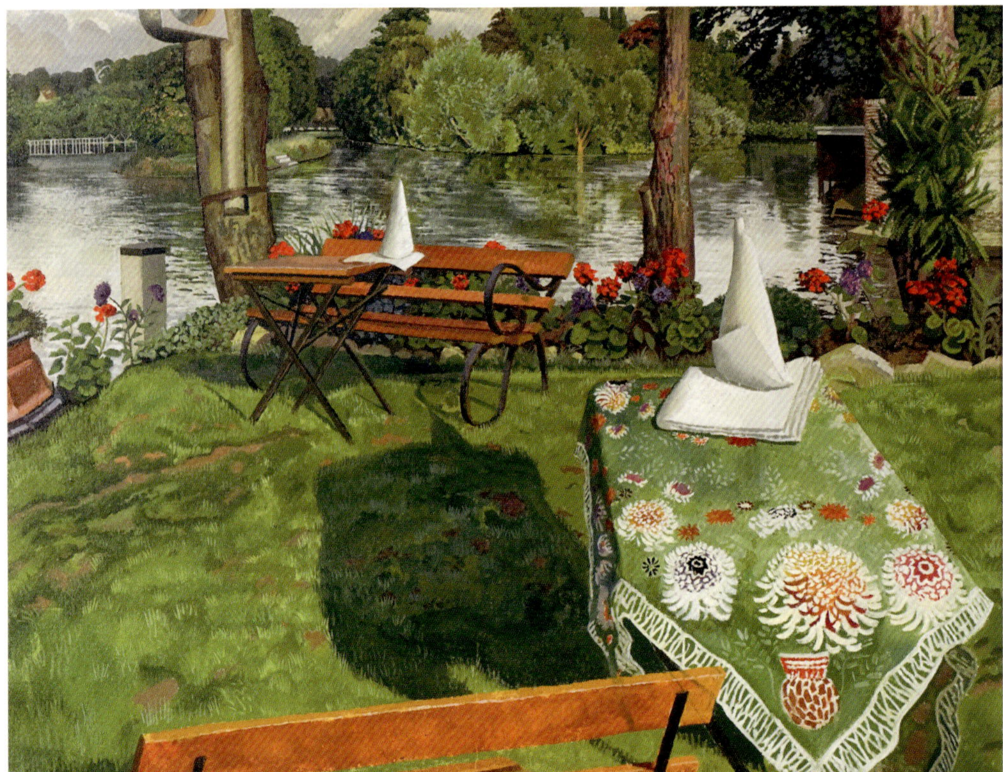

3
STANLEY SPENCER
Ferry Hotel Lawn, 1936
Oil on canvas, 71 x 94 cm
Dundee Art Gallery

December 1918 he was back in Cookham, at work on the painting, which recalled in vivid detail one of his experiences as a medical orderly, *Travoys with Wounded Soldiers arriving at a Dressing-Station at Smol, Macedonia* (1916, Imperial War Museum). Meanwhile, upstairs in Fernlea, Spencer found his unfinished canvas of *Swan Upping*, begun in 1915 (Tate). In a conscious effort to pick up where he had left off, "to recover my lost self", as he put it, he completed the painting in 1920. He then embarked upon a series of New Testament scenes, beginning with *The Last Supper* (Stanley Spencer Gallery, Cookham), based on a drawing he had made in a malthouse in 1915, which he also completed in 1920. This was followed, over the next three years, by *Christ's Entry into Jerusalem* (1920, City Art Gallery, Leeds) via Cookham High Street, *The Betrayal* (fig. 36), a haunting, nocturnal encounter in the alley between the gardens of Fernlea and The Nest, and *Christ carrying the Cross* (1920, Tate) along the now familiar Via Crucis. Only the *Crucifixion* he painted in 1921 (Aberdeen Art Gallery and Museums) makes specific reference to his wartime experiences, to "the memory I had of some mountain which was in a range ... dividing Macedonia from Bulgaria", but there can be little doubt that all of these pictures were related to the need he felt, like so many survivors of that war, to come to terms with the immediate past and, at the same time, to celebrate his homecoming.

In 1923, Spencer was staying with his friend the painter Henry Lamb, who described him in a letter to his future brother-in-law as "sitting all day evolving acres of Salonica and Bristol war compositions". Some of those drawings survive and what they show is that by the time Spencer showed them to Louis and Mary

Behrend, who were among his earliest patrons, he had worked out a detailed scheme to commemorate his war, and to redeem his fallen comrades, in a purpose-built chapel based on the design of Giotto's Scrovegni Chapel in Padua. When the Behrends gave him the chance of a lifetime to realise his ambitions, as a memorial to Mrs Behrend's brother who had fallen in Macedonia, his reaction was "What ho! Giotto!" Meanwhile, Spencer had become engaged to another painter, Hilda Carline, whom he married in 1925. Their union, together with its impact on 'Cookham', is summarized in the painting he completed a year later and exhibited in 1927, his *Resurrection, Cookham* (1924–26, Tate). This vast canvas (274 × 549 cm) could be described as Spencer's spiritual autobiography to date. By his mid thirties, he had enjoyed early success as an artist, survived the horrors of war, and found happiness and sexual fulfilment in married life. Yet he could not help contrasting Cookham with his loss of innocence in both war and love, and he was determined to reconcile the conflict in a defiant pictorial affirmation of faith in his birthplace as Eden-on-Thames. Inevitably, then, Spencer depicted the ultimate Resurrection on the Day of Judgement as taking place in the churchyard there. Into this timeless allegory of redemption, he introduced his new family, the Carlines, and welcomed them to salvation. The painting was not only received favourably, it was described by Fry as "a very personal conception carried through with unfailing nerve and conviction", and it was bought at once by the Duveen Fund for the Tate Gallery.

The Resurrection, Cookham was a deliberate prelude, a kind of ritual purification, prior to Spencer turning his attention to the commission he had received from the Behrends, to decorate what was to become the Sandham Memorial Chapel, built to his specifications. In 1927 Stanley and Hilda Spencer moved with their baby daughter Shirin to Burghclere, where the Behrends had built them a house close by, appropriately called Chapel View, so that the artist could set to work on his cycle of wartime reminiscences. Within the bay divisions of the north and south walls, Spencer described his own experiences, at the Beaufort Hospital and on the Macedonian front. Many of them were mundane, reflecting the drudgery and boredom of everyday, army life as opposed to the horrors of war, but Spencer recalled them in almost obsessive detail, painting his comrades in arms not as other war artists had done, like Nevinson, who deliberately reduced the soldiers in his painting of *Returning to the Trenches* (1914–15, National Gallery of Canada, Ottawa) to moving parts in a vast war machine, but as individuals who defied regimentation to wash their clothes in mountain streams, to pick and eat berries from the bushes, and to throw themselves down on the ground, exhausted after a route march. The sacrifice made by many of them is all the more poignantly reflected in the painting of *The Resurrection of the Soldiers* (1928–29) that fills the east wall. Here, it is the men themselves who rise up from their graves to pile their standard issue, plain white crosses above the actual altar, beside which several of them appear to stand, life-sized and uncannily present in the intimate space of the chapel. "The Burghclere memorial ... redeemed my experience from what it was," Spencer explained, "namely something alien to me."

In 1932, shortly before he completed his paintings for the chapel, Spencer moved with his family back to Cookham, where he was able to afford a large, semi-detached house, Lindworth, some fifty yards away from his childhood home. In the same year he became an Associate of the Royal Academy and was invited to exhibit in the British Pavilion at the Venice Biennale. As if to relax from the travails of his war paintings, Spencer also produced a series of freshly observed landscapes, including *Cottages at Burghclere* (fig. 4), with their bosky front gardens divided by neatly clipped hedges and white picket fences. That ability to capture and convey the essence of rural England was a talent he shared not only with contemporary painters like the Nash brothers, but also with poets and musicians, such as Edward Thomas and Percy Grainger.

By Spencer's own account, "all the figure pictures done after 1932 were part of some scheme", whose purpose was to reclaim Cookham as the earthly paradise in which innocence and experience were reconciled and the sacred reunited with the profane. The materiality of this second "chapel in the air" or "Church-house" as he called it, is open to question; he described the village street of Cookham as "the Nave and the river which runs behind the street [as] a side aisle". Within it, however, in his mind at least, Spencer gave pride of place to such paintings as *The Dustman*, or *The Lovers* (fig. 5) in which "the joy of his bliss is spiritual in his union

4
STANLEY SPENCER
Cottages at Burghclere, 1930
Oil on canvas, 62.2 × 160 cm
Fitzwilliam Museum, Cambridge

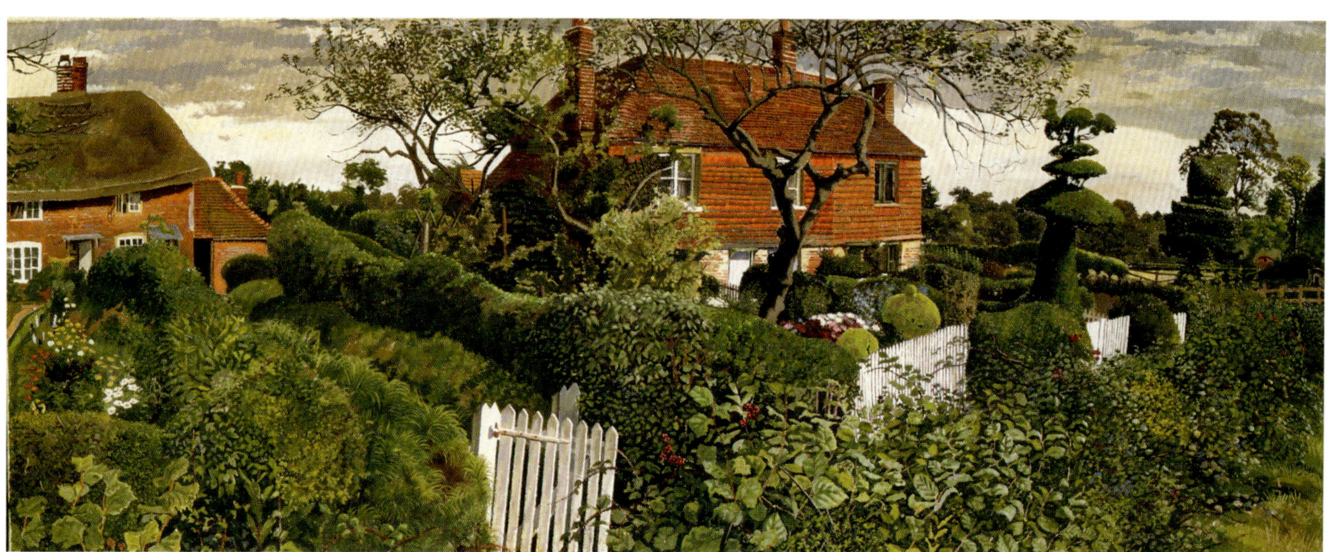

5

STANLEY SPENCER

The Dustman, or **The Lovers**, 1934

Oil on canvas, 114.9 x 122.5 cm

Laing Art Gallery, Newcastle upon Tyne

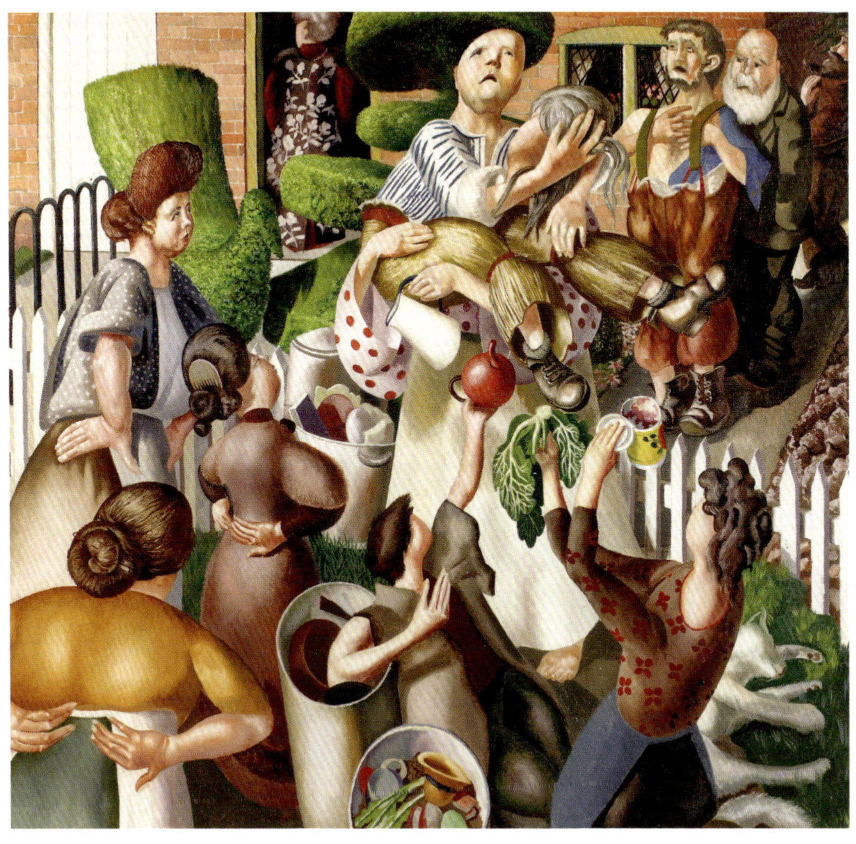

with his wife who carries him in her arms and experiences the bliss of union which his corduroy trousers quicken". Their ecstasy is witnessed by "other reuniting wives of old labourers" who hold up as offerings the contents of the dustbins: "And so I resurrect the teapot, and the empty jam tin, and the cabbage stalks, and as there is a mystery in the Trinity, so there is in these." The voice is that of an evangelist for sexual freedom whose paintings, like the novels of D.H. Lawrence (an expurgated edition of *Lady Chatterley's Lover* was published in 1932), challenged conventional attitudes to both art and life. In *Love Among the Nations* (1935, Fitzwilliam Museum, Cambridge) Spencer traced the origins of his faith in universal love back to "the war, when I contemplated the horror of my life and the lives of those with me, I felt that the only way to end the ghastly experience would be if everyone suddenly decided to indulge in every degree and form of sexual love". His own prominence in this multi-racial love-in anticipates his appearance alongside Preece in the sexually exposed and highly charged double portraits he painted of them both at a time when he aspired to enjoy relations simultaneously with not one but two wives. The outcome was perhaps inevitable, leading to the rueful admission in 1938 that "my desire to paint is caused by my being unable – or being incapable – of fulfilling my desires in life itself".

By the end of that decade, Spencer was estranged from both women; he had been threatened with prosecution for obscenity; he had resigned from the Royal Academy; and even his most loyal patrons, including Edward Marsh, were unimpressed by his recent work. Today, the *Couples* he painted in his series, *The Beatitudes of Love* (1937–38), seem overwhelmingly of their period, comparable in many respects to the work of the German Expressionists and of Max Beckmann in particular. But at the time they found little or no favour. When Marsh saw them at Dudley Tooth's gallery, they "fogged his monocle"; according to Spencer "He had to keep wiping it and having another go". To Spencer's question, "What's the matter with them?" he could only splutter, "Terrible, terrible, Stanley". Yet at the same time Spencer painted a succession of landscapes in that familiar vein of softly sunlit naturalism which was guaranteed, unlike his subject pictures, to find a ready market. In deliberate contrast, paintings like *Cookham Moor* (1937, Manchester City Art Gallery) and *Gardens in the Pound* (fig. 6) are uncomplicated by the inclusion of figures to distract the attention of the viewer from their eerie stillness. Only the open door in *Greenhouse and Garden* (figs. 7, 9), beyond the strings of onions hanging from the rafters, hints at "footfalls echo[ing] in the memory". Dismissive as Spencer could be of his "potboilers", it is hard to believe that he did not derive considerable comfort, as well as pleasure, from these timeless moments of horticultural contemplation.

In 1940 Spencer found employment for the second time in his career as a war artist. His initial suggestion that he should paint a Crucifixion with a predella depicting scenes from the invasion of Poland was met with embarrassed silence. Instead he accepted the invitation to visit the shipyards of Port Glasgow to record the war effort there. Auspiciously, he wrote to Hilda soon after his arrival to tell her that "I like it here, being lost in the jungle of human beings, a rabbit in a vast rabbit warren". After a period of relative isolation, he found himself in an environment which must have been strangely reminiscent of his life in uniform. Like the soldiers beside whom he fought, he saw the workmen in Lithgow's shipyard as an army of individuals. Crouching beside them in the confined spaces in which they riveted and welded, he captured them by the light of their acetylene torches to produce an extraordinary series of industrial scenes which bear comparison only, and favourably, with the murals of Diego Rivera. In October 1940 they were an instant success when the first of them were exhibited in the War Artists' Exhibition at the National Gallery, London. Spencer had, once again, redeemed his lost self.

He repaid Port Glasgow in the currency he knew best. He recalled,

> One evening, when unable to write due to a jazz-band playing in the drawing-room just below me, I walked up along the road past the gas works to where I saw a cemetery on a gently rising slope .... I seemed then to see that it rose in the midst of a great plain and that all in the plain were resurrecting and moving towards it .... I knew then that the Resurrection would be directed from this hill.

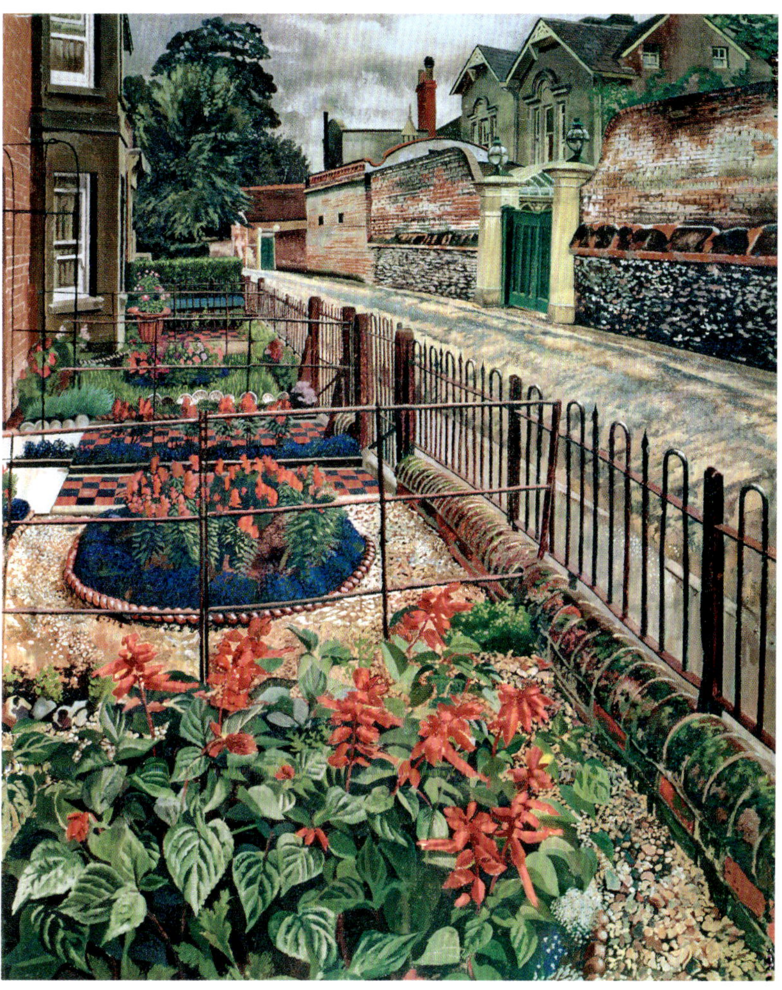

6
STANLEY SPENCER
Gardens in the Pound, 1926
Oil on canvas, 91.5 x 76.2 cm
Leeds City Art Gallery

From that point onwards, the war artist deferred to the visionary and Port Glasgow joined Cookham among the suburbs of heaven. Resurrections followed in rapid succession (see fig. 14), culminating in the vast canvas depicting *The Resurrection: Port Glasgow* by which Churchill was so underwhelmed in 1950.

In November of that year, Hilda died. In spite of, or possibly because of, his mistreatment of her, Spencer refused to acknowledge that fact, and for the remaining nine years of his life he maintained a constant stream of one-way correspondence with her. His painting *Love Letters* (1950, Thyssen-Bornemisza Collection, Lugano) pays posthumous tribute to what amounted to an obsession. So too does *Love on the Moor* (1949–54, Fitzwilliam Museum, Cambridge), in which Hilda is elevated to the status of the rather buxom and slightly embarrassed young twentieth-century Venus of Cookham. Spencer completed that final tribute to his birthplace as the modern Eden in 1955, by which time he was living, creatively, in and from the past. His last great cycle of post-modern testaments was both retrospective and valedictory. With instant recall, he returned to the scenes of his Edwardian youth to represent *Christ preaching at Cookham Regatta* (1959, Stanley Spencer Gallery, Cookham) on a text he prescribed: "I believe Christ talking is really me love-making to everybody."

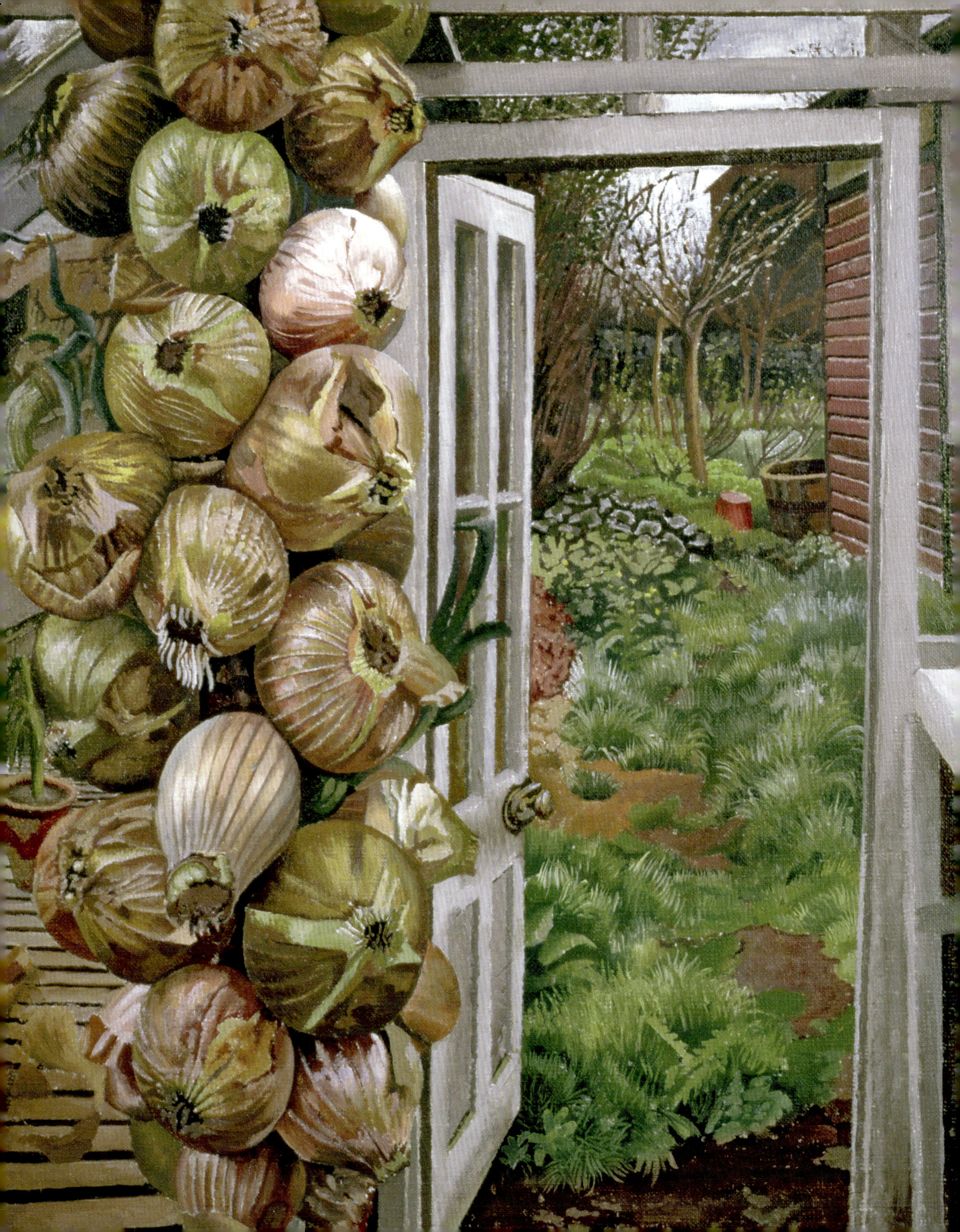

STANLEY SPENCER'S GARDENS

Keith Bell

> In this painting [*By the River*, 1935, University College, London] the people are doing nothing in particular which gives a better opportunity of conveying the essential atmosphere of the place. Neither the chestnut trees in the distance, nor the near shrubs are doing anything; they are all just "being".[1]

> At this time of year I usually concentrate on some aspect of landscape which includes flowers as the time of their duration is short. This landscape therefore is a garden plot.[2]

From the beginning of his career, Stanley Spencer's landscape, garden and flower paintings were the most popular aspect of his artistic production. In terms of sales and critical reception, these paintings – particularly those dating after 1929 – represented for many the high point of his work, while the figure paintings were often considered to be stylistically awkward and difficult to understand. Spencer's persistent complaint that landscape painting was an impediment to the production of the figurative works which were more important and meaningful to him did not deter dealers and collectors from concentrating enthusiastic attention on, and paying good prices for, representations of Cookham and the English countryside. Art historians, on the other hand, for a long time largely ignored the landscapes, choosing instead to concentrate mainly on the figurative paintings with their complicated iconographies and powerful imagery. Only in the past two decades or so has more attention been paid to the stylistic development and critical reception of Spencer's landscapes.[3] Similarly, while landscapes have usually been included in considerations of Spencer's work, there have seldom been exhibitions dedicated purely to the landscape, garden and flower paintings. (The excellent shows at the Stanley Spencer Gallery in Cookham have been a welcome exception.)

The exhibition of Spencer's garden paintings at Compton Verney is an important addition to Spencer studies, because it gives us an opportunity to consider these works as an ensemble, rather than as punctuation marks between the figure paintings. Spencer himself made no distinction between his landscape, garden and flower paintings, referring to all of them simply as "landscapes". Except in the early years, when he painted a number of what might be called 'true' landscapes (for example, *Cookham*; 1914, Tullie House Museum and Art Gallery, Carlisle), Spencer's paintings were predominantly hybrid in appearance, with foregrounds often crowded with flowers and shrubs, and a longer view of the landscape opening out beyond, as in *Bellrope Meadow* (fig. 8) This essay seizes

/
STANLEY SPENCER
Greenhouse and Garden, 1937
Detail of fig 9

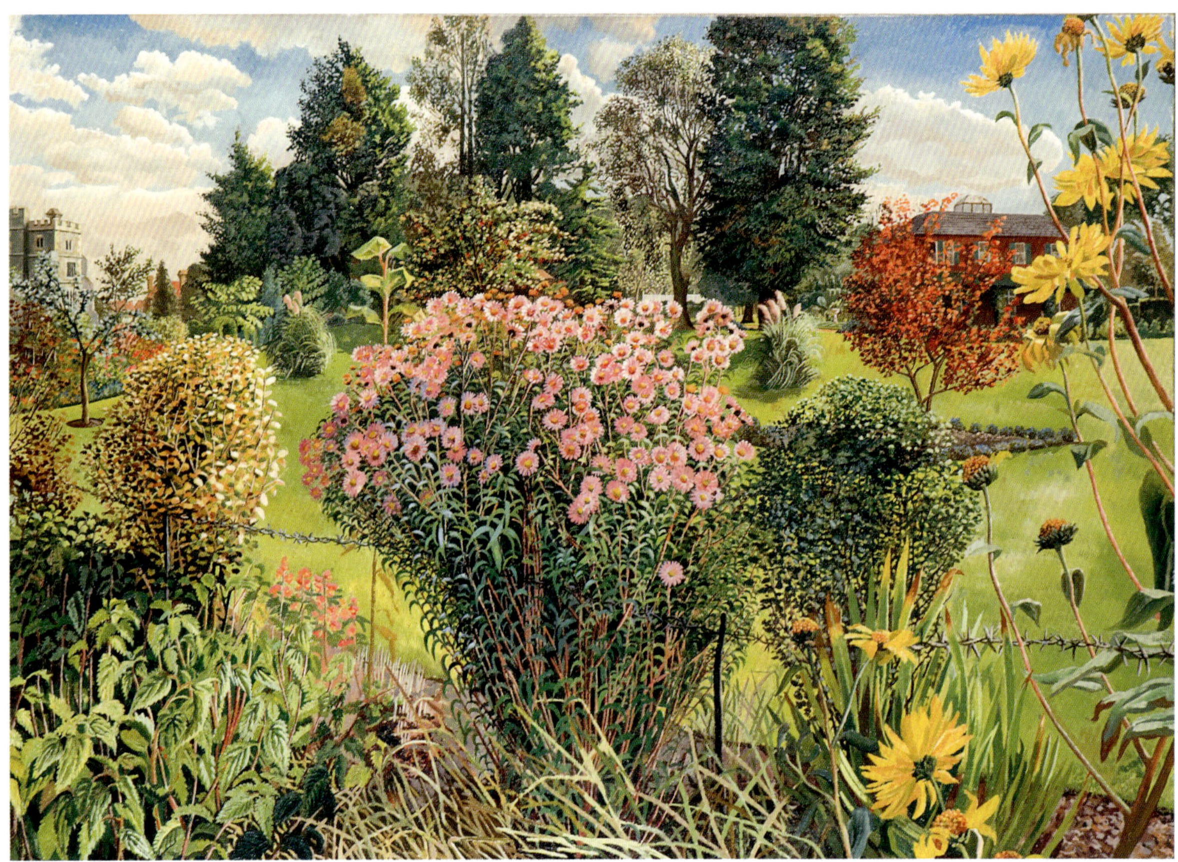

8
STANLEY SPENCER
Bellrope Meadow, 1936
Oil on canvas, 91.5 × 129.5 cm
Rochdale Art Gallery

the chance not only to consider the landscape paintings as a discreet body of work but also to focus on the origins of Spencer's landscape manner, its place in the history of English painting and Spencer's undoubtedly ambiguous attitude to the genre. In addition, we will consider Spencer's relationship with his dealer, Dudley Tooth, which illuminates the business of producing and selling landscape paintings in the years between 1932 and the artist's death in 1959.

Contemporary critics often detected a European influence in Spencer's landscape work. And it is true that his lifelong devotion to Cookham and the wider English countryside can be compared to the similar attachment of the European Impressionists, notably Berthe Morisot, Claude Monet and Camille Pissarro, to painting flower gardens (often their own), parks and those particular spaces, neither entirely urban nor totally rural, which formed the new and rapidly expanding suburban periphery of the big European cities. Occupied by the new middle classes, these spaces were often also homes to the artists who depicted them, as well as providing the community of patrons who bought many of their landscape and garden pictures. Pissarro, in particular, had begun exploring the possibilities of these modernizing landscapes by painting the London suburbs of Upper Norwood and Sydenham in 1870, and Bedford Park and Chiswick in 1897. Cookham, of course, was also one of these liminal spaces, thanks to a commuter service from London, established in 1854, that quickly transformed what had been a quiet Thames-side village into a dormitory for city professionals. Like his French compatriots, Spencer found both subject-matter and purchasers in his local village for many of his lush suburban landscapes and flower paintings.

It was this subject-matter – the suburban garden landscape – that set Spencer apart from many of his contemporaries in England, including, for example, the brothers John and Paul Nash, Henry Lamb, Vanessa Bell, Duncan Grant and Roger Fry, all of whom were tied to a more traditional notion of what constituted a landscape. All the same, Spencer's approach to landscape, in particular, his intimate and often spiritual connection to his immediate environment, drew heavily on English precedents. John Constable's renderings of the Suffolk countryside and his family home, notably views like *Golding Constable's Kitchen Garden* and *Golding Constable's Flower Garden* (both 1815, Ipswich Museums and Galleries), as well as the cloud studies painted in his garden in Hampstead, are early examples of an artist working within the familiar boundaries of his day to-day existence. Constable's depiction not only of picturesque subjects but also of the more prosaic side of country life, such as his family's kitchen garden, is frequently reflected in Spencer's paintings, for example, in works like *Greenhouse and Garden* (figs. 7, 9), *The Marrow Bed* (1926, private collection) and *The Hoe Garden Nursery* (fig. 10).

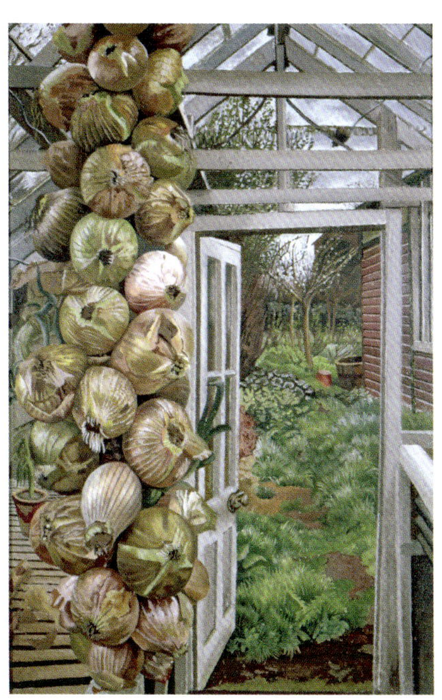

9
STANLEY SPENCER
Greenhouse and Garden, 1937
Oil on canvas, 76.2 x 50.8 cm
Ferens Art Gallery, Hull

Constable was certainly not alone as an English source for Spencer's work. For example, the visionary overtones of his domestic landscapes are reminiscent of the work of Samuel Palmer, who lived and painted for several years in the Kentish village of Shoreham. Influenced, like Spencer, by the Italian 'Primitive' painters of the fifteenth and sixteenth centuries, Palmer created religious pictures such as *A Hilly Scene* (*c.* 1826–28, Tate), which were set in the countryside around Shoreham, an area that Palmer considered his "Valley of Vision". In the same way, the village of Cookham became the centre of Spencer's spiritual universe.

Spencer also had a connection with the Pre-Raphaelite painters, a group to which he was often compared. Here the influences ran deep. Spencer's brother Will visited William Holman Hunt in his studio, and Spencer owned an illustrated art book on Dante Gabriel Rossetti published by Gowans & Gray, which he acquired in 1913. A reproduction of John Everett Millais's *Ophelia* (1852, Tate) hung in Fernlea, the Spencer family home. Like many other works by the Pre-Raphaelites – for example, Holman Hunt's *Our English Coasts* (1852, Tate) and Ford Madox Brown's *An English Autumn Afternoon* (1852–53, Birmingham City Art Gallery) – Millais's *Ophelia* is emphatically set in the English landscape. This setting, together with the minute attention to detail and the care with which the plants and bushes are recorded, clearly influenced Spencer's landscape and figurative work. So did Millais's habit, shared with the French Impressionists, of working

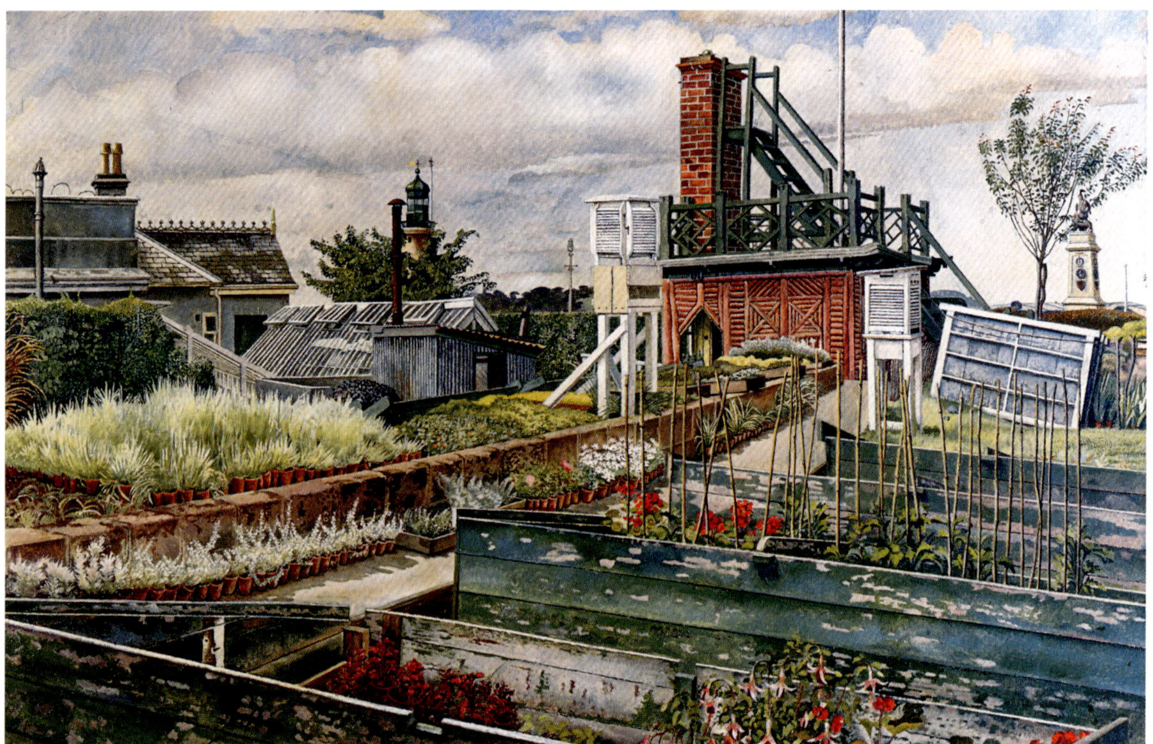

10
STANLEY SPENCER
The Hoe Garden Nursery, 1954
Oil on canvas, 67.8 × 108.2 cm
Plymouth City Museums and Art Gallery

en plein air, a practice adopted by Spencer for his landscapes around 1905 when the teenaged artist found inspiration "sitting among the hollyhocks and runner beans"[4] as he drew Sandall's Cottage.

Between December 1935 and January 1940, Spencer made a list of some of his earliest artistic references.[5] The artists in this eclectic catalogue, all of whom are English, include Heath Robinson, the cartoonist and illustrator 'Dicky' Doyle (probably his fairy illustrations), a volume of the *Royal Academy Illustrated*, a picture of Br'er Rabbit from W.T. Stead's *Books for the Bairns* series, which Spencer liked for its "homely quality", and Helen Stratton's illustrations for an edition of Hans Christian Andersen's *Fairy Tales*. Spencer also listed E.H. New's illustrations to Gilbert White's *Natural History of Selborne*, a work that inspired him to "draw a dead thrush" and a "dried up frog" which he felt to be "part of the garden". White's *Natural History*, with its numerous plates, provided Spencer with an early notion of how he might similarly represent the gardens and fields around Cookham.

Together with a variety of literary subjects ("some attempts to draw Br'er Rabbit"),[6] the young Spencer began producing garden and landscape studies in pen between 1905 and 1908, including *Meadow, Willow, Stream and Footbridge* (1905); *Silver Birch near Vicarage* (*c*. 1905); *The Cedar, Cookham* (*c*. 1905); *Mrs East's Cottage* (1907) and *Cockmarsh from the Hill* (*c*. 1906), many of which were to become subjects for oil paintings later in his career. The rigorous formal training and wider knowledge of the art world that Spencer acquired at the Slade School of Fine Art, which he attended from 1908 to 1912, later augmented this combination of literary and artistic influences. Together, these experiences almost immediately culminated in a series of superb religious paintings, all set in Cookham. They include *The Nativity* (1912, Slade School of Fine Art); *The Visitation* (1912–13, private collection), with its view through the schoolroom door towards the sheds of the King's Arms and the roof of Lindworth; and *Zacharias and Elizabeth* (1914, Tate), which shows the garden of St George's Lodge and Cliveden Woods as seen from the back window of Wisteria Cottage.

As Spencer recalled in 1937, *Zacharias and Elizabeth* brought together the familiar rhythms of everyday life with intense spiritual awareness:

> A version of the St Luke passage, the gardener dragging the branch of ivy, and Mrs Gooden giving me permission to walk about the garden of the untenanted St George's Lodge, resulted in this painting .... The whole of what I hoped was dependent on the reality of everyday life.[7]

This composition was also the prototype for many subsequent figure paintings and, especially, for Spencer's garden scenes. In *Zacharias and Elizabeth*, Spencer used an elevated viewpoint looking down into the garden (a figure at the left of the painting also peeps over the garden wall), with a view extending into the distance at the top of the composition. The figure on the left acts as a kind of proxy for the viewer who uses his vantage point to witness the events taking place in the secret garden. Spencer referred to this as the "feeling of wonder at what was on the other side".[8] Cookham is a maze of narrow lanes, walls and hedges partly concealing houses and gardens, and Spencer's desire to look over walls recalls his childhood explorations of the village.

The artist used similar compositions for *The Betrayal* (second version; fig. 36) and *Neighbours* (fig. 11), the latter being a version of an illustration for the month of April commissioned for the 1927 edition of the Chatto & Windus Almanack. This publication also contains several other 'peeking into' views, including a scene (September), of the Spencer children picking walnuts from a tree that overhung their schoolroom in the back garden of Fernlea. Spencer used an elevated viewpoint once again for a number of the Burghclere Chapel paintings (discussed later on), notably *Convoy of Wounded Soldiers arriving at Beaufort Hospital Gates* (1927), which, despite its military subject, is awash with flowering rhododendrons that crowd in on the open-topped buses.

The First World War and military service in Bristol and Macedonia broke the spell of curiosity and wonder that had permeated Spencer's youth. If anything, Spencer's experience of war heightened his affinity with his home village of Cookham. The intensity of this connection was best expressed through his correspondence with the artist Desmond Chute, an associate of the sculptor Eric Gill and a member of the Guild of Saint Joseph and Saint Dominic at Ditchling in Suffolk, who later went on to become a Catholic priest. Chute visited Spencer at Beaufort War Hospital, Bristol, in 1916, where the artist worked as an orderly in

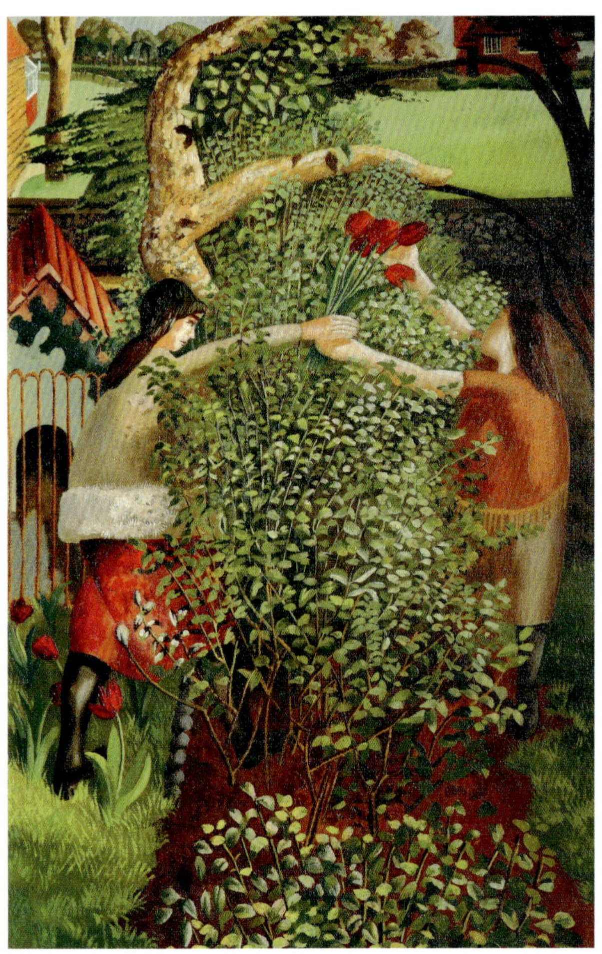

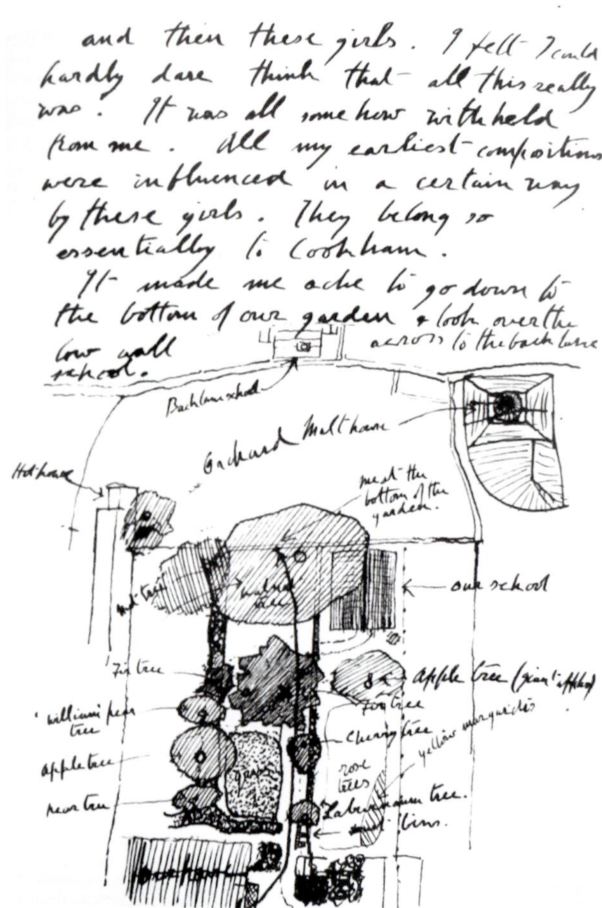
and then these girls. I felt I could hardly dare think that all this really was. It was all somehow withheld from me. All my earliest compositions were influenced in a certain way by these girls. They belong so essentially to Cookham.
It made me ache to go down to the bottom of our garden & look over the low wall across to the back lane school.

the Royal Army Medical Corps. Their subsequent relationship was an important one for Spencer, who found the well-educated and intellectual Chute to be both a sympathetic listener and an important source of spiritual and literary sources and ideas. Their correspondence (now in the collection of the Stanley Spencer Gallery), shows Spencer at his most self-consciously literary, as he sets out to convey his feelings for Cookham to his friend in a series of long, poetic descriptions, often intense and dreamlike, sometimes mixed with prosaic comments about the landscape. These two modes of feeling jointly inform us about the way Spencer approached the best of his garden and landscape paintings throughout his career.

On returning from military leave to Cookham in June 1916, for example, Spencer told Chute how "it made me ache to go down to the bottom of our garden [at Fernlea] and look over the low wall across to the back lane school". A map of the garden accompanies the description, with annotations identifying the trees: "William pear tree", "laburnum tree", "apple tree (giant apples)", "Cherry tree", "fir tree", "rose trees" (fig. 12). And in another letter of 1916, this time written from Salonica, Spencer wrote how he imagined walking through the village upon his return from the war:

11
STANLEY SPENCER
Neighbours, 1936
Oil on canvas, 76.2 x 50.8 cm
Stanley Spencer Gallery, Cookham

12
STANLEY SPENCER
Letter to Desmond Chute, June 1916
Stanley Spencer Archives, Cookham

> Then I get up and look out of the dining room window down our garden and over the gardens on either side of us and over a big orchard at the bottom of the garden but I am more particularly looking at the yew tree which is framed by the walnut tree forming the background. This fir tree has many apertures, openings which greatly excites [*sic*] my imagination. They all seem holy and secret.

Not surprisingly, Spencer returned home profoundly disturbed by his wartime experiences, causing him to claim that he had been "crushed by the war"[9] and consequently would never be able to paint with the clarity and intensity that he had achieved in the pre-war works. Following a period working in Cookham, he lived a peripatetic life, staying with artist friends including Henry Lamb, Muirhead Bone and the Carline family in Hampstead. In 1925 he married Hilda Carline and in the following year he completed *The Resurrection, Cookham* (Tate), in which the lush flowers and shrubs play a major role in setting the mood for the miraculous occasion. Later, in 1927, he moved to Burghclere to paint the scenes for the Oratory of All Souls Sandham Memorial Chapel, which were completed in 1932.

During those same years leading up to 1932, Spencer painted numerous landscapes, both in Cookham and in a number of other rural venues, including Durweston, Petersfield and Wangford. For the most part, Spencer's paintings were fairly traditional landscape views of the southern English countryside, in works like *A Farm in Dorset* (1920, private collection) and *Landscape with Cultivator* (1920, lost). Often he worked in company with his brother Gilbert or with friends like Henry Lamb, John and Paul Nash and Sydney and Hilda Carline. At the same time, he also began to step outside the standard, picturesque views of the countryside to include the rougher, more unkempt aspects of rural life, in paintings such as *Tree and Chicken Coops, Wangford* (1926, Tate), *Turkeys* (1925, Tate), and *The Red House, Wangford* (fig. 13). In this last work, he opted to paint a recent farm labourer's house rather than a more romantic vernacular building or one of the nostalgic cottage scenes that had been made popular at the turn of the century by Helen Allingham.

Meanwhile, Spencer's landscape paintings were becoming sought-after items among both his friends and a wider audience. At his one-man exhibition at the Goupil Gallery in 1927, he sold eleven out of the twelve landscapes listed in the catalogue, at prices which compared favourably to those fetched by his figurative works – £65.5s for *Stinging Nettles* (1926, private collection), for example, compared to £68.5s for the early figure painting *Joachim among the Shepherds* (1913, National Gallery and Museum, Wellington). As a consequence of these sales, Spencer came to realise that landscape painting provided his best chance of making a living from his art. At the same time, however, he could also see that landscapes alone could not satisfy his desire to paint. As he commented later about this period: "I had no wish or intention ever to be fully expressive by means of painting an object in front of me."[10]

Spencer further analysed his ambiguous feelings about landscape painting in a letter dated 17 November 1927 to his friend and confidant Desmond Chute:

> This stinging nettle one [*Stinging Nettles*, painted at Wangford, Suffolk] is more imaginative as a composition [than some of the other paintings]. I had real feelings about it and something is growing in me as a result of having painted it, this last fact is what has made me feel that my desire to be able to paint a landscape is not without some reason.

A few lines later, however, he again expressed doubts about working directly from the subject: "It is strange that I feel so 'lonely' when I draw from nature but it is because no sort of spiritual activity comes into the business at all." He continued: "Its [*sic*] this identity business. There are certain things where I can see and recognize clearly this spiritual identity in something, but if I am drawing and don't see this clearly its [*sic*] all up." In other words, he preferred the figure paintings, the "John Donnes" and "Joachims", in which "this miraculous spiritual meaning [could] change the boredom of drawing into a tremendous experience".

Despite this important misgiving, Spencer did achieve a certain level of satisfaction from his landscape paintings, perhaps more than he was usually willing to admit. This is clearly apparent in an early masterpiece, *Cottages at Burghclere* (fig. 4), painted in 1930 and an early example of the artist's mature landscape style. In this painting, Spencer was able to convey the voluptuous excess of summer, with the garden flowers and lopsided topiary almost overwhelmed by the weeds and brambles pressing against and spilling over the white picket fences. As I have suggested elsewhere,[11] this combination of nature and human presence is also brilliantly described in Thomas Hardy's Wessex novels, notably *Tess of the d'Urbervilles* (1891).

While some critics praised Spencer for the modern, European tendencies of his work, others – particularly the more conservative voices – appreciated what they saw as the 'Englishness' of his landscapes and garden scenes. In 1930, a critic in *The Times* described *Cottages at Burghclere* as "the work of a Pre-Raphaelite who has looked at Cézanne", going on to declare: "Without for a moment disparaging the intelligent application of lessons from France ... it may be questioned if Mr Spencer is not showing a better way in working towards unity through what may be called the rough of his native talents." Although this was not the only possible reading of Spencer's originality and influences, nonetheless it was the perceived Englishness of his landscapes that made them such a success in the art market. Early in 1932 Spencer's dealer, the owner of the Goupil Gallery, William Marchant, died. Although the gallery struggled on under Mrs Marchant's management, many of its artists began to find dealers elsewhere. In March of that year, Dudley Tooth of Arthur Tooth & Sons approached Spencer and, in October, he agreed to join

13
STANLEY SPENCER
The Red House, Wangford, 1926
Oil on canvas, 50.8 × 76.2 cm
Ferens Art Gallery, Hull

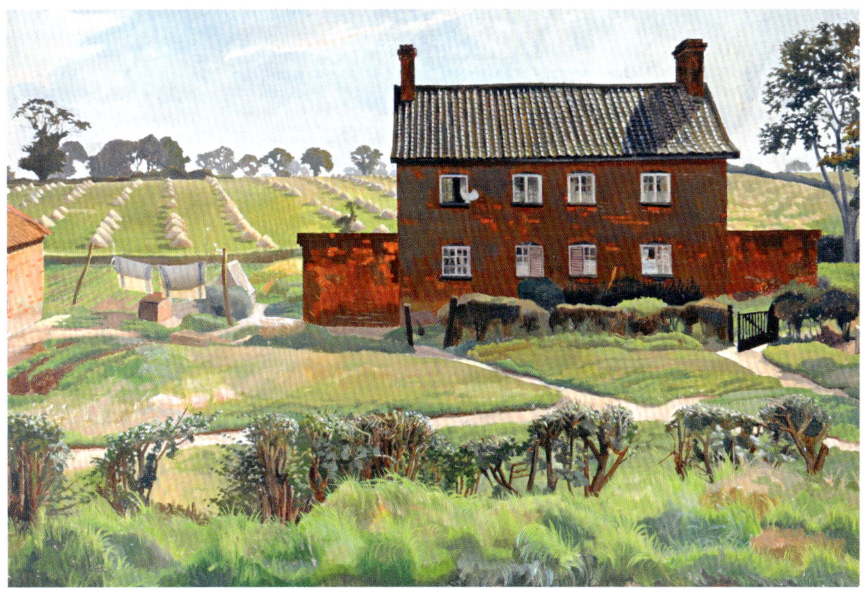

Tooth's on the usual financial terms of thirty-three and a third per cent. The relationship between dealer and artist was on the whole a highly successful one, and if Spencer complained occasionally to friends that Dudley Tooth pushed him too hard to produce paintings and, in particular, landscapes, on the whole the relationship proved profitable for both parties. Tooth was willing to exhibit and attempt to sell Spencer's increasingly 'difficult' figure paintings, so long as the artist was willing to produce landscapes and still lifes – the easy sellers – at the same time.

As Tooth remarked to Spencer in a letter of May 1933: "Your landscapes are much liked and therefore I would not advise you to neglect them altogether this summer as I think a variety of subjects is an excellent thing."[12] Tooth had begun his letter by reporting the sale of *Villas at Cookham* (1932, Walker Art Gallery, Liverpool) to the Contemporary Art Society for £85, thereby providing a useful reminder of the financial advantages to be gained from landscape and still-life painting. His letter was in response to one from Spencer, received earlier that day, in which the artist suggested that it "would be better" if he devoted "less time to landscapes and more time to what I enjoy doing such as the old woman in black [*Sarah Tubb and the Heavenly Visitors*; fig. 37]."

Spencer's objections to producing landscapes in quantity reflected several concerns. The first of these was born of a growing preoccupation with his standing as an artist in the British art world in the two decades following the First World War. The critical success of his first one-man show at the Goupil Gallery in 1927 and the purchase of *The Resurrection, Cookham* (1924–26) by the Tate Gallery, followed by the triumph of the Sandham Memorial Chapel at Burghclere, saw Spencer established in a relatively prominent position among interwar British figurative painters. This status seemed to be confirmed in 1932 by his election as an Associate Member of the Royal Academy and the inclusion of five paintings and five drawings among the works exhibited in the British Pavilion at the Venice Biennale that same year.

Yet despite this generally enthusiastic response to his figurative work, the display of a dozen landscape and garden paintings at his Goupil show had attracted the interest not only of private collectors but also of art dealers and public art institutions. These paintings, invariably devoid of the sometimes strange figures and unusual narrative elements that provoked a certain amount of negative critical comment, were on the whole easier to understand in the familiar context of English landscape painting. Furthermore, they were comfortably 'local', even conventional, when seen alongside the work of Spencer's contemporaries, English modernists like Paul Nash or Vanessa Bell with their provocatively avant-garde stance. In the frequently conservative art world of the interwar years, Spencer's landscapes appeared 'modern' but not radical.

Despite the general approbation, some critics were dismissive of the artist's landscape work. Reviewing Spencer's major one-man exhibition at Tooth's in 1936, Anthony Blunt described the landscapes as fillers, "which seem to be included just to show that he can paint prettily if he wants to".[8] The critic for the *Scotsman* was much more generous, and his perceptive comments clearly sum up the more common views of the people who bought Spencer's landscapes over most of his career:

> Personally I think Spencer is in the tradition of British Pre-Raphaelitism ... the poetic naturalistic kind of Hunt, Brown and the young Millais. Spencer paints landscape as they did, not so minutely of course, but with the same prodigious delight in all the facts of nature for their own sake. He loves to paint nettles and grasses leaf by leaf, blade by blade, as they did. He loves it all too much to leave anything out.[14]

Spencer's reluctance to spend too much time on landscape paintings was now further challenged by Tooth's considerable success in placing these very works with public institutions. As well as selling *Villas at Cookham* (1932) to the Contemporary Art Society, Dudley Tooth also sold *Terry's Lane, Cookham* (1932) to the Tate Gallery, *Alpine Landscape* (1933) to the Vancouver Art Gallery and *Madonna Lilies* (1935) to Leeds City Art Gallery. Meanwhile, Kenneth Clark, newly appointed Director of the National Gallery, acquired *White Lilac* (1934) for his own collection. By May 1935, Tooth was reporting to Spencer that he had "three Public Galleries wanting me to let them know when you have finished any new landscapes".

Responding to this request, Spencer laid out his concerns to Tooth in a letter of 12 June 1933, commenting anxiously:

> As I feared every one as usual wants my landscapes and no one wants the more imaginative and characteristic work I do. I am very sorry public galleries are taking my landscapes as representative works of mine. Except the Tate there is only one public gallery (Belfast) which owns a picture [*The Betrayal*, second version; fig. 36] by me: a thoroughly representative work of mine full of the qualities

> which I know are the only things I have truly felt I meant. The other Galleries own landscapes and it gives me no pleasure and I feel no pride to think that they own them. And if people praise my landscapes I would rather not be told.

Later, in July of that year, in a letter reporting the completion of *Madonna Lilies*, Spencer went a step further when he asked Tooth to avoid selling the painting to a public gallery. He wrote: "If you could find a private purchaser I would prefer it to a gallery one as I still vainly hope that the galleries may have work that really represents my art." In the event, however, *Madonna Lilies* was purchased by Leeds City Art Gallery and there is no further evidence that Spencer tried to direct the placement of his paintings.

Together with his concerns about their placement, Spencer was also more disturbed than ever by the growing pressure from both galleries and now private collectors to ramp up production of landscapes and still lifes. The appearance of these paintings at prestigious venues such as the Venice Biennale and the Royal Academy – *The Angel, Cookham Churchyard* (1933, private collection), for example was shown at the RA in the summer of 1934 – broadened his public exposure and pushed up his prices. Interested buyers had only to walk ten minutes from the Academy to Tooth's premises on Bond Street to view more work. *The Angel, Cookham Churchyard* sold directly from the Royal Academy exhibition and a few months later Tooth was appealing to Spencer for similar paintings. "[I] look forward to receiving the two landscapes as soon as possible as I think I can place them for you", he wrote on 22 October, and again in a telegram on 12 December: "When will two new landscapes be ready. Urgently needed Tooth."

To further complicate matters, Spencer was becoming increasingly reliant on producing landscapes, garden scenes and still lifes for the majority of his income. On the domestic side, he needed to support a family that now included two daughters, Shirin, born in 1925, and Unity, born in 1930. Furthermore, following the completion of the Burghclere Chapel in 1932 and consequently the end of the Behrends' patronage, Spencer had bought a house, Lindworth, in Cookham, using up most of the proceeds of his recent sales. Early evidence of money concerns appears in a letter from Tooth to Spencer of 8 July 1932: "It may relieve your financial worries if I tell you that both landscapes are sold .... Several clients who called too late to buy pictures, are disappointed and therefore I can sell other landscapes as soon as you get them ready." Joining Tooth's undoubtedly provided Spencer with a welcome structure for economic survival, but, as the Spencer-Tooth correspondence shows, the association left Spencer with less time than he had hoped in which to carry out his post-Burghclere plans.

This is not to say that Dudley Tooth forced Spencer to neglect the work the artist felt to be central to his practice, including a series of scenes for the Church

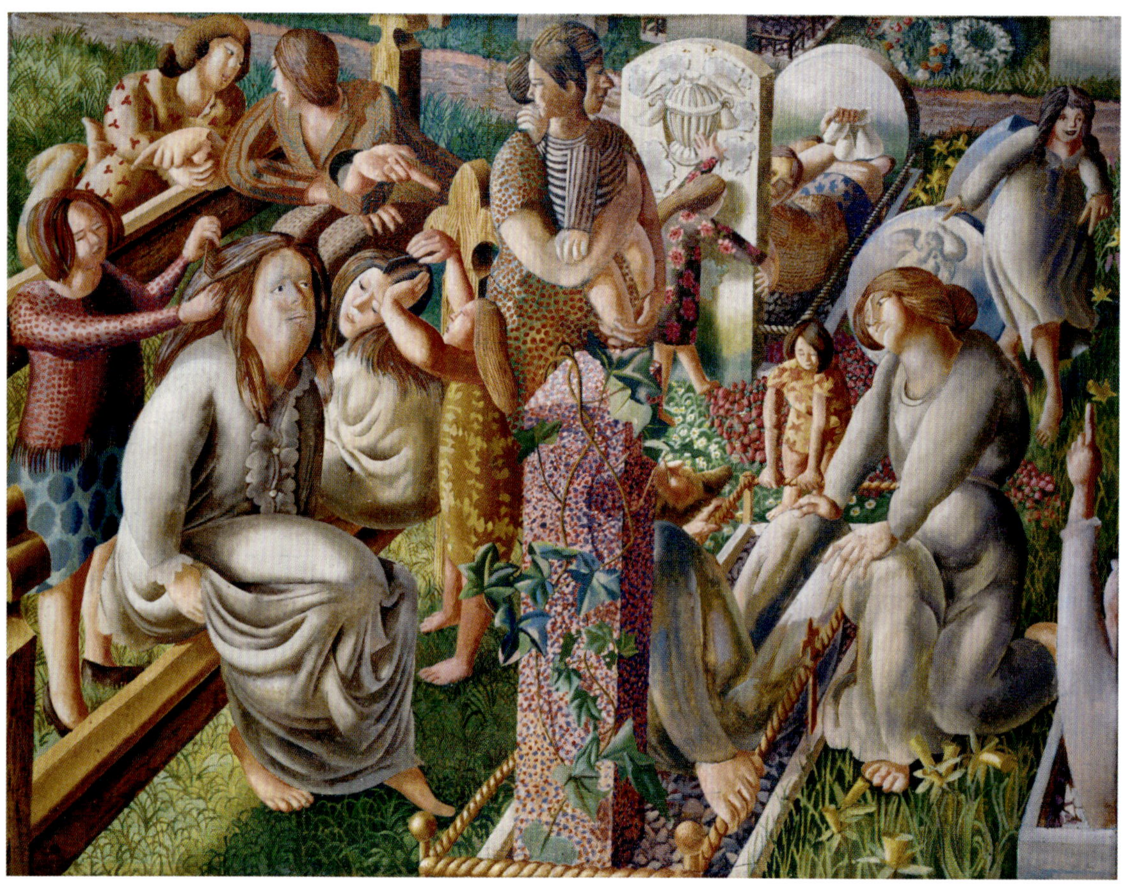

14
STANLEY SPENCER
Resurrection: Tidying, 1945
Oil on canvas, 79.2 × 101.6 cm
Birmingham City Art Gallery

House that was already forming in Spencer's mind as the Burghclere project drew to a close. Tooth has sometimes been accused of impeding Spencer's creative progress and dictating what he should paint. However, a close reading of the correspondence between artist and dealer suggests that, while Tooth was at times demanding when it came to the production of landscape and garden paintings, he was also diligent in trying to sell the figurative works and willing to exhibit them at every opportunity. This was evident after the rejection by the Royal Academy hanging committee of *The Dustman*, or *The Lovers* (fig. 5), and *Saint Francis and the Birds* (1935) when the paintings were submitted for inclusion in the summer exhibition of 1935. Spencer resigned from the RA in protest, but Tooth was quick to exploit the subsequent publicity by exhibiting the rejected works in his gallery (a sort of Salon des Refusés) and he soon sold *Saint Francis* to the Tate, with *The Dustman* subsequently going to the Laing Art Gallery in Newcastle.

Despite some early disagreements, Spencer and Tooth eventually came to an unwritten arrangement whereby the artist would concentrate largely on garden scenes, landscapes and flower paintings during the spring and summer seasons when it was possible to paint outdoors. In reality, as Spencer's finances deteriorated in the mid 1930s, he could be found working on landscapes at all times of the year. For example, the two garden paintings, *From the Artist's Window,*

Cookham, a view of the back garden of Lindworth, and *Flowers and Rooftops* (both 1938, Carrick Hill Collection, Adelaide), painted in March and sold in April 1938, were views from the inside looking out, a splendid solution to the problems caused by the vagaries of the early spring weather.

In 1941, when Tooth was engaged in war work, and Richard Smart temporarily took over management of the gallery in his place, communications were usually based on gentle persuasion rather than outright entreaties. Thus, in a letter of 1 April Smart suggested diplomatically that Spencer might begin to work again on some garden paintings:

> I am wondering if you like it and have the time [if] it would be possible during the Spring and early Summer to produce some of those little flower pictures that people have always liked so much. This is only a suggestion as I am not one to prescribe what any artist should paint.

And again in 1945, Smart told Spencer:

> Do not think of painting landscapes unless you want to. Keep on with the canvases that really interest you [almost certainly the Port Glasgow Resurrection series; see fig. 14] and that you want to get done for your show.

When Tooth returned to the gallery, he continued the search for a solution to the landscape versus figure painting dilemma, hoping to find an arrangement that would please both dealer and artist, and at the same time maintain a steady stream of picture sales. In 1950, following Spencer's reinstatement to the Royal Academy, Tooth wished to send the fine painting *Garden Path, Cookham Rise* (1949, private collection), to the summer exhibition at the "request" of the President, Sir Gerald Kelly. Spencer was exhibiting his Port Glasgow Resurrection canvases at the same venue and clearly did not want to have a garden work distract attention from the Glasgow paintings, his first major figurative sequence since the completion of the Shipbuilding on the Clyde project in 1946.

Tooth's solution, which he outlined in a letter to Spencer on 3 March, was to show both *Garden Path* and the Resurrection paintings, but only "on the understanding that it [*Garden Path*] would be hung in a different room to the Resurrection pictures". He concluded with the sly remark that "It is bound to sell there and I shall put the price up £50 (to £300) for all the trouble they have given you [over the 1935 rejection of Spencer's paintings and his subsequent resignation from the RA]".

Although Spencer never fully embraced the idea of producing landscapes in large numbers, he eventually became resigned to this necessary routine, as he ruefully admitted to his friend, Marjorie Metz, in June 1954: "Any way I set to and began doing my usual landscapes, and I am now in the midst of doing three ... I need to paint 20 to 30 landscapes [per year] and to keep that up non stop for ever

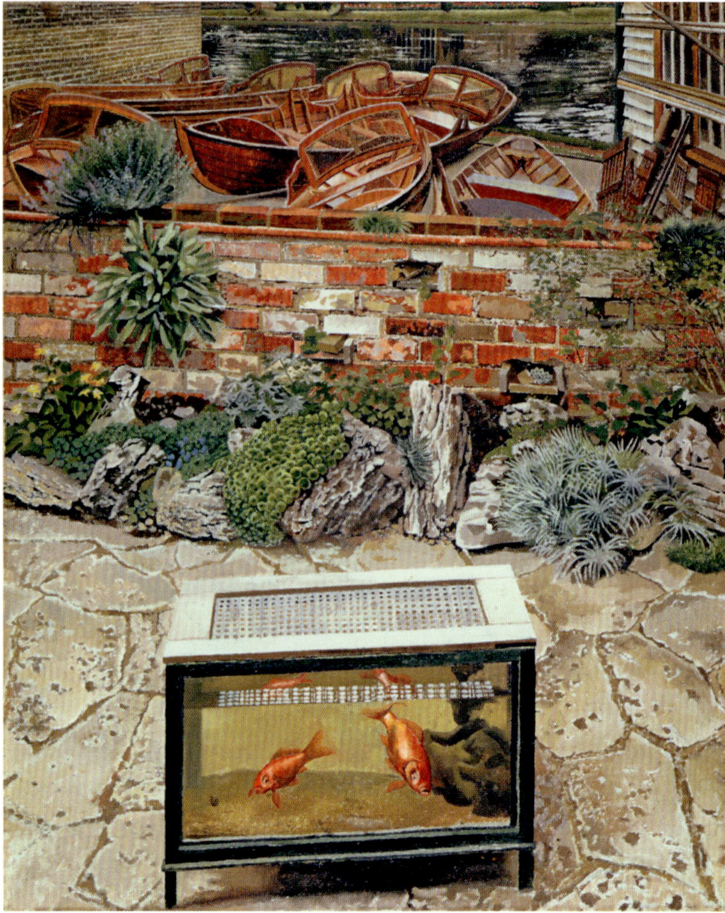

15
STANLEY SPENCER
Boatbuilder's Yard, Cookham, 1936
Oil on canvas, 86 x 71 cm
Manchester City Art Gallery

more." And earlier, in a 1936 notebook entry, he established a plan to spend substantial parts of the summer months painting outdoors:

> In a weeks time I will finish Tree landscape. Aug 15 – Sept 10. I will in the morning do a big view, and in afternoon do the Cookham Rise Cottages now just begun. Then I will do Odney Club with leaves turning in morning and view from Mr Wiggs in afternoon and the ducks in yard also when I can.[15]

Not surprisingly some of the paintings that resulted from these campaigns were less than perfect, but on the whole Spencer maintained a remarkably consistent standard, even at times when, as in the 1930s, the pressure to produce in order to pay off his debts was extreme. Fine paintings like *The Boatbuilder's Yard, Cookham* (fig. 15), *Bellrope Meadow, Cookham* (fig. 8) and *Gardens in the Pound, Cookham* (fig. 6) were just a few of the garden subjects he painted during the summer of 1936.

In what is probably the best description of Spencer's painting activities around Cookham, the artist wrote to Dudley Tooth on 5 February 1935:

> About the landscape you have [*Rowborough, Cookham*, 1934, private collection] .... What happened was this. I was painting that landscape when Mrs Corble, a part of whose garden appears in the landscape came up to me and asked, after looking

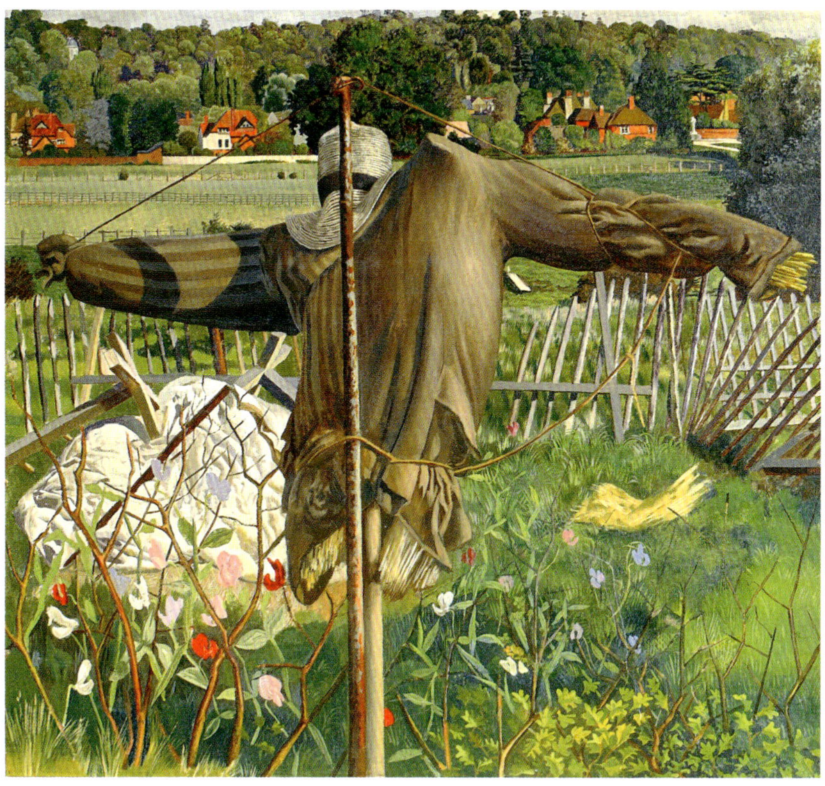

16
STANLEY SPENCER
The Scarecrow, Cookham, 1934
Oil on canvas, 71.1 x 76.2 cm
Stanley Spencer Gallery, Cookham

> at it if she might have it. I then informed her that my landscapes were all rather expensive and that I should want £125, and she said "That's alright, do let me have it" and so it was settled. Then I had intended to do this Scarecrow which I had been gazing at for days while I was doing this landscape and as soon as it was done I began the scarecrow landscape.

In a note written in 1938, Spencer described *The Scarecrow, Cookham* (fig. 16) in evocative terms:

> Left and deserted as it was it seemed daily to become more a part of its surroundings. It was like watching a person slowly changing into a part of nature. And I liked the feeling of it always being there ... in the evening he faded into the gloaming like [a] Cheshire cat.[16]

In a curious example of the crossover between his garden paintings and his figurative works, Spencer almost immediately reused the scarecrow scene as the basis for a commissioned Crucifixion, with the figure of the scarecrow transformed into that of the crucified Christ and the distant view of Cookham more or less repeated.

Spencer's oft-remarked reliance on direct observation when working on the garden and landscape compositions frequently caused him difficulties when the seasons changed and the blossoms faded and died. In a letter to Tooth (26 May 1943), Spencer gave a humorous description of his experiences while painting outdoors:

> In my landscape, I am tucked away in a deserted corner of a Cookham meadow where there is a maytree, stinging nettles and wild flowers. One of these maytrees was dying off when I got to it, so of course, needless to say, soon after I had started, the place was visited by men who are dashing all over the place in queer shaped vehicles [on a military exercise], but my plot is still alright. As soon as they were gone, I thought "Now all is quiet" but when I went up yesterday, I listened and paused on my way there; whence cometh then this bleating in my ear? As a grim visaged Samuel I approached. The vast field was white in the sun with sheep and lambs.

In a similar vein, Jane Martineau, daughter of Jack and 'Cash' Martineau, Taplow residents and Spencer's friends and patrons, vividly described watching Spencer at work on *Rock Roses, Old Lodge, Taplow* (private collection) in 1957:

> He did the picture of rock roses, because I happened to see it, over about ... eight, nine weeks. During that time first of all there'd be tulips out, and they died. They're in the picture. And then the rock roses came out, and they died, and then the roses came out, and so everything comes into the picture. It became superimposed, layer upon layer, as to what was flowering over eight or nine weeks.[17]

Spencer returned to live in Cookham in 1932, after an absence of nearly eleven years. One of his first tasks after he settled in was to develop plans for what he wished to paint after the completion of the Sandham Memorial Chapel. The Burghclere paintings had been conceived a decade earlier, and since then he had produced few entirely new compositions, with the exception of five works commissioned by the Empire Marketing Board and a number of garden paintings and landscapes. In addition, as he was to continue to complain for the rest of his life, his traumatic war experiences in Bristol, and especially in Macedonia, had ruptured the sense of homely bliss that had led to the extraordinary creativity of the years 1908 to 1915.

Fortunately, his experience at Burghclere provided a model on which he could build. The design for the Memorial Chapel had been inspired by his admiration for the narrative paintings of the early Italians – Giotto's Scrovegni Chapel in Padua, and Masaccio's Brancacci Chapel and Fra Angelico's paintings in the Friary of San Marco, both in Florence, all of which he had studied from the illustrations in his collection of Gowans & Gray art books. Back in the comfortable familiarity of his native village, he planned to bring together, or "marry" as he put it, the old childhood atmosphere of Cookham with his more recent, adult life and experiences of love and marriage with his wife Hilda in a series of painting cycles loosely united under the broad title of *The Last Day*, or *The Last Judgement*, in which Cookham was to be transformed, almost imperceptibly, into a village in heaven.

In order to keep the plan coherent, the paintings were to be hung in a notional building which he named the Church House. This architectural setting was the outcome of an idea developed at Burghclere, when he had imagined expanding the chapel paintings into the almshouses that flanked the memorial. Unlike the chapel at Burghclere, however, the Church House was not even remotely feasible. Still, it provided Spencer with an imagined structure for his mythopoeic imagery, which he laid out in numerous notebook drawings and which remained the subject of his figurative paintings until his death in 1959.

While Spencer's preoccupation with the Church House paintings might suggest a substantial divide between the figurative and landscape works after the completion of Burghclere in 1932, in practice the two areas were in some ways very closely related. Given the constraints of time, Spencer developed the habit of painting landscapes and garden views of Cookham, which he also used as settings for the Church House paintings. In fact, he often worked on the two concurrently. In this way, the subject of *Cookham Moor* (1937, Manchester City Art Galleries) was also the site for the big figurative painting *Love on the Moor* (1949–54, Fitzwilliam Museum, Cambridge), a celebration of his love for Hilda, begun in 1937 and completed in 1955, and *Cows at Cookham* (1936, Ashmolean Museum, Oxford), a painting derived from one of the illustrations he made for the 1927 Chatto & Windus Almanack. As Spencer later said of *Cookham Moor*, "If and when I have in some picture ... expressed more fully all I feel about a place such as this then I feel happy in doing a landscape of such a place",[18] a clear indication that, despite the never-ending pressure to produce paintings in volume, at least some garden paintings and landscapes, in particular the ones set in Cookham, did hold an importance for Spencer that reached beyond simple representation.

The new figurative paintings, like their precursors, were also rooted in the Cookham landscape. In the same way that *Christ carrying the Cross* (1921, Tate) was set in the street outside Fernlea, the Church House paintings, like *A Village in Heaven* (1937, Manchester City Art Galleries), were set in and around the village, in this case Cookham Moor and the war memorial. Gardens appear frequently in paintings such as *The Dustman*, or *The Lovers* (fig. 5), and *Neighbours* (fig. 11), which featured the back garden at Fernlea and showed Spencer's sister exchanging gifts over the privet hedge with a cousin who lived next door (a memory from his childhood). Yet other paintings directly addressed Spencer's relationship with his ex-wife Hilda, who had died in November 1950. In *Hilda with Bluebells* (1955, private collection), Spencer painted an evocative scene set on Hampstead Heath, depicting Hilda gazing Madonna-like at a clump of bluebells, while the artist sprawls on the grass next to her.

Gardens also played a prominent role in figure paintings set outside Cookham, including the Port Glasgow Resurrection series where the graveyard, like that depicted in *The Resurrection, Cookham* (1924–26, Tate), was filled with beds over-flowing with flowers and flowering shrubs (see fig. 14). A garden world of colour

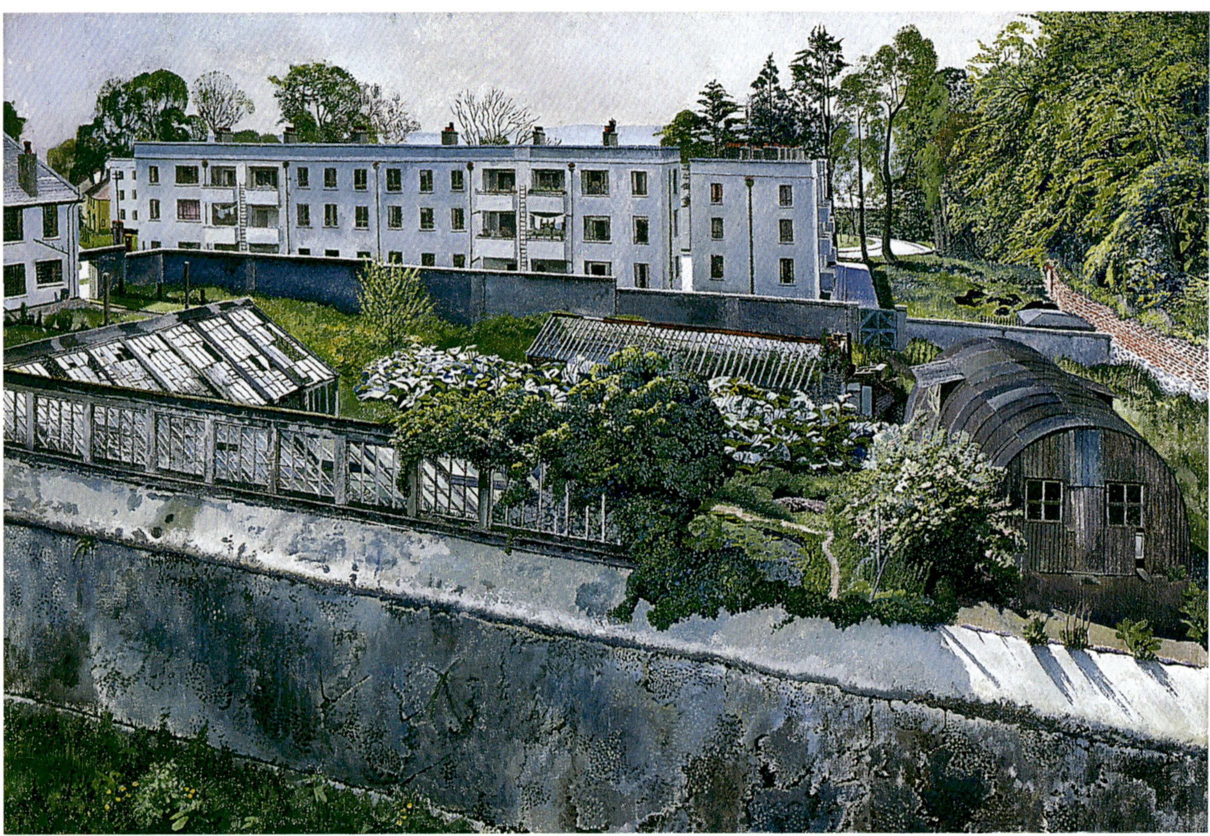

17
STANLEY SPENCER
Merville Garden Village near Belfast, 1951
Oil on canvas, 59.5 x 91 cm
Dunedin Public Art Gallery, New Zealand

and fragrance greets the newly resurrected as they rise from their graves and prepare to begin life in heaven. Reporting to Dudley Tooth in October 1944 from his lodgings with Mrs Whitford in Glencairn, Port Glasgow, at a time after most flowers were over for the season, Spencer told his dealer that he had uncharacteristically used photographs of his landscapes and flower paintings, supplied by Tooth, in order to get the painting done: "In this flowerless place (only at present) I managed primroses, ivey [*sic*] that creeps around among the grass, violets, and convolvulus, and daisys [*sic*]."

While painting the Resurrection pictures, Spencer was also at work on a landscape, "a very fine distant view [through] chestnut, holly, yew, and big bushes and shrubs", of *Port Glasgow from Clune Brae* (1944, private collection). This painting took Spencer only two weeks to complete compared with his more usual average of four to six, "a test for time ... as the leaves were falling".

At the same time Spencer was painting views of carefully tended gardens, flower beds and landscapes, although he also continued to paint the kind of scruffy back gardens and farmyards he had first begun to produce between the wars. These paintings, including fine canvases like *The Hoe Garden Nursery* (fig. 10), *Goose Run, Cookham Rise* (1949, private collection) and *Merville Garden Village near Belfast* (fig. 17), were all painted using the same intimate detail and canvas size as the more conventional garden scenes, but with rusty corrugated-iron sheets, pieces of wood, weedy vegetable patches and broken greenhouse windows taking the place of manicured flower beds and carefully trained creepers. In *The Scrap Heap* (1944, Art Gallery of New South Wales, Sydney), which was painted in between work on the Shipbuilding on the Clyde series in Port Glasgow, Spencer went a step further, by depicting a kind of industrial 'garden' of discarded, rusty steel cut-outs and girders, roughly stacked in a corner of the shipyard. While some of these paintings were no doubt the result of expediency – the scrap heap, for example, was next to the ships that were his main subject – they represent a considerable departure from standard notions of what might constitute a garden and as such are an important contribution to the genre in England.

During the period between the completion of the chapel at Burghclere and his death in 1959, Spencer's popularity as a painter of garden and flower pictures continued to grow. This was due to the skilful salesmanship of Dudley Tooth, together with the responsiveness of the English public to paintings that were undoubtedly of high quality. Like the best of Spencer's figure paintings, his garden landscapes succeeded through their searching re-examination of familiar places and objects, an extraordinary control of space, and an ability to draw the viewer into looking again at everyday scenes that might otherwise had received no more than a passing glance. Stylistically, the paintings of this period are relatively consistent, with fences, walls or foliage pushing up against the picture plane, causing the viewer to experience the subject from the exact position occupied by the painter. In this way, Spencer establishes a degree of intimacy between artist and viewer, and viewer and subject, which is not usually found in garden paintings.

As time went on, Spencer's flower paintings and the foregrounds of his garden paintings, like *Greenhouse and Garden* (fig. 7), became increasingly detailed, so that they often have the visual immediacy of Dutch seventeenth-century still lifes – the indoors brought outside. While the thinner paint surface of the later paintings has sometimes been compared unfavourably to the richer brushwork and more opaque paint of the pre-war subjects, the quality of Spencer's garden, flower and landscape paintings remained consistently high throughout. This is apparent, for example, in one of his last major garden paintings, appropriately a view of *The Churchyard, Cookham* – or as Spencer called it in a picture list, *Cow Parsley, Cookham Churchyard* (1958, private collection) – which the artist donated in aid of the restoration of Cookham Church.

In Spencer's paintings every nettle, every bean, every tulip has the potential to be more than it seems while remaining exactly what it is. Although Spencer's gardens may have been "potboilers", as he sometimes disparagingly called them, they came from the hand and eye of a visionary artist with a fierce attachment to the countryside around him. Welcome to Stanley Spencer's garden.

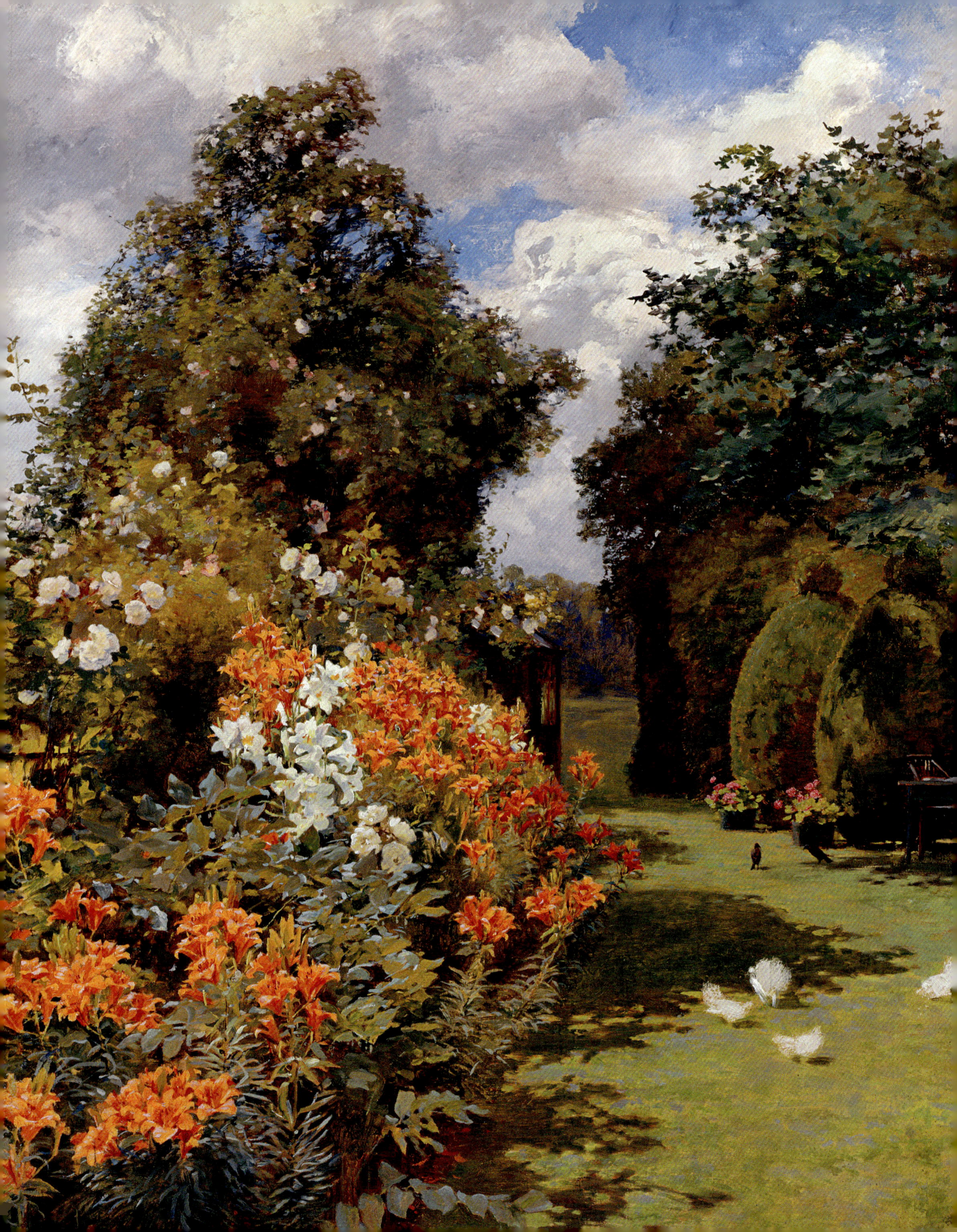

"HAPPY ENGLAND": THE ARTIST AND THE GARDEN FROM ALLINGHAM TO SPENCER

Martin Postle

In 1891, the year of Stanley Spencer's birth, the Fine Art Society mounted an exhibition of paintings by the artist and gardener Alfred Parsons (1847–1920). Henry James, who was invited to write an introductory essay, entitled 'Gardens and Orchards', observed that "it would be strange if the words 'happy England' should not rise to the lips of the observer of Alfred Parsons's numerous and delightful studies of the gardens, great and small, of his country".[1] Today Parsons is largely forgotten, but in the latter years of the nineteenth century he was a major force in promoting the aesthetic of the specifically English garden, as a painter and as a garden designer. Ironically, however, it was through his contacts with a group of well-heeled émigré American artists and writers that Parsons made his mark. In the postcard-pretty village of Broadway in the Cotswolds, Parsons developed his friendship with the American artists and writers Edwin Austin Abbey and Frank Millet, in whose garden John Singer Sargent composed his celebrated painting, *Carnation, Lily, Lily Rose* (1886, Tate). Along with Sargent, Abbey, Millet and Parsons, the Broadway clique included Henry James, the poet Edmund Gosse and the American Shakespearian actress Mary Anderson. As well as designing gardens for the wealthy aesthetes of Broadway, including Anderson, Parsons eventually created his own garden there around his house, Luggers Hall, designed in the Arts and Crafts style by the Scots architect Andrew Prentice. In 1911, the same year that his house was built, Parsons submitted his diploma picture to the Royal Academy, *Orange Lilies, Broadway* (fig. 18), an image which epitomized the kind of "happy England" which his garden art and garden design represented.

A few years earlier, in 1903, eighty watercolours of gardens by another prominent garden artist, Helen Allingham, were published in a book entitled *Happy England*. In the opening years of the twentieth century, happiness in England was synonymous with the garden. And, although Allingham was herself rather unhappy about the book's title – since her garden paintings were restricted to a small area of south-east England – she was aware that her modest pictures of rural gardens, like those of Parsons, represented the quintessence of what many regarded as a specifically English (as opposed to British) national identity. While Alfred Parsons was well connected in sophisticated international social circles, Helen Allingham was perhaps a less likely focal point of the new English garden aesthetic. Born Helen Paterson, in Swadlincote, Derbyshire, Allingham was influenced in her artistic aspirations by her aunt, Laura Herford, the first female artist to gain entry to the Royal Academy schools. Working initially as a book and magazine illustrator, Allingham took up watercolour in the 1870s, following her

18
ALFRED PARSONS
Orange Lilies, Broadway (detail), c. 1911
Oil on canvas, 92 × 66 cm
Royal Academy of Arts, London

marriage to the poet, William Allingham, and their move the following decade to the hamlet of Sandhills, near Witley, Surrey. From here she began her second career as a prolific painter of cottage gardens in Surrey, Sussex and Kent, although she did range as far as Middlesex, Berkshire and the Isle of Wight.

Allingham's paintings typically depict cottages with thatched or red-tiled roofs, often in a state of semi-dilapidation, with blooming gardens and frequently inhabited by young women carrying laundry or a child (fig. 19). Her rural idyll can be traced back to the picturesque aesthetic of the later eighteenth century. However, as the scholar Anne Helmreich has observed, the popularity of Allingham's garden paintings was also bound up with the more recent gentrification of the English village – particularly in the south-east – as poets, artists and aesthetes took advantage of the new lines of communication introduced by the railway and gravitated towards rural properties within commuting distance of the capital.[2] Through her husband, Allingham began to socialize with leading literati, including Alfred Lord Tennyson, Robert Browning, Thomas Carlyle and John Ruskin, the last of whom expressed particular admiration for her work.[3] In 1886 the Fine Art Society mounted a one-woman show of her paintings, entitled *Surrey Cottages*, and in 1890 she became the first female member of the Royal Society of Watercolours. During Stanley Spencer's formative years, the influence of Allingham's art upon perceptions of rural homes and gardens was pervasive, and while she painted only occasionally in Berkshire, many people during the early years of the twentieth century would no doubt have viewed the attractive village of Cookham and its cottage gardens through Allingham's rose-tinted spectacles.

At the same time that Allingham was popularizing the cottage garden through her art, new approaches to gardening were giving legitimacy to the 'wild' rural garden as a site for aesthetic and artistic creativity. At the forefront of this pioneering spirit in English garden design was an Irish gardener, William Robinson, who conceived of cottage gardens as "little Elysiums".[4] In 1870 Robinson challenged the orthodoxy of the formal Victorian garden aesthetic through his book *The Wild Garden*, for which Alfred Parsons supplied the illustrations. Robinson believed that the garden should above all look natural and be filled with colour, using native plants rather than exotic species raised in hothouse environments. The following year Robinson founded his own journal, *The Garden*, which included contributions from prominent writers such as John Ruskin and William Morris. Although Robinson was a gardener first and foremost, he did more than anyone to bring together artists and gardeners in a common cause, united by their mutual love of colour in nature. He was an admirer of Alfred Parsons, and encouraged his ambitions as a garden designer. Robinson's most distinguished protégé was, however, Gertrude Jekyll, another artist-cum-garden designer.

19
HELEN ALLINGHAM,
Cowdray Cottage,
c. 1880–1900
Watercolour, 34.5 x 38.8 cm
British Museum, London

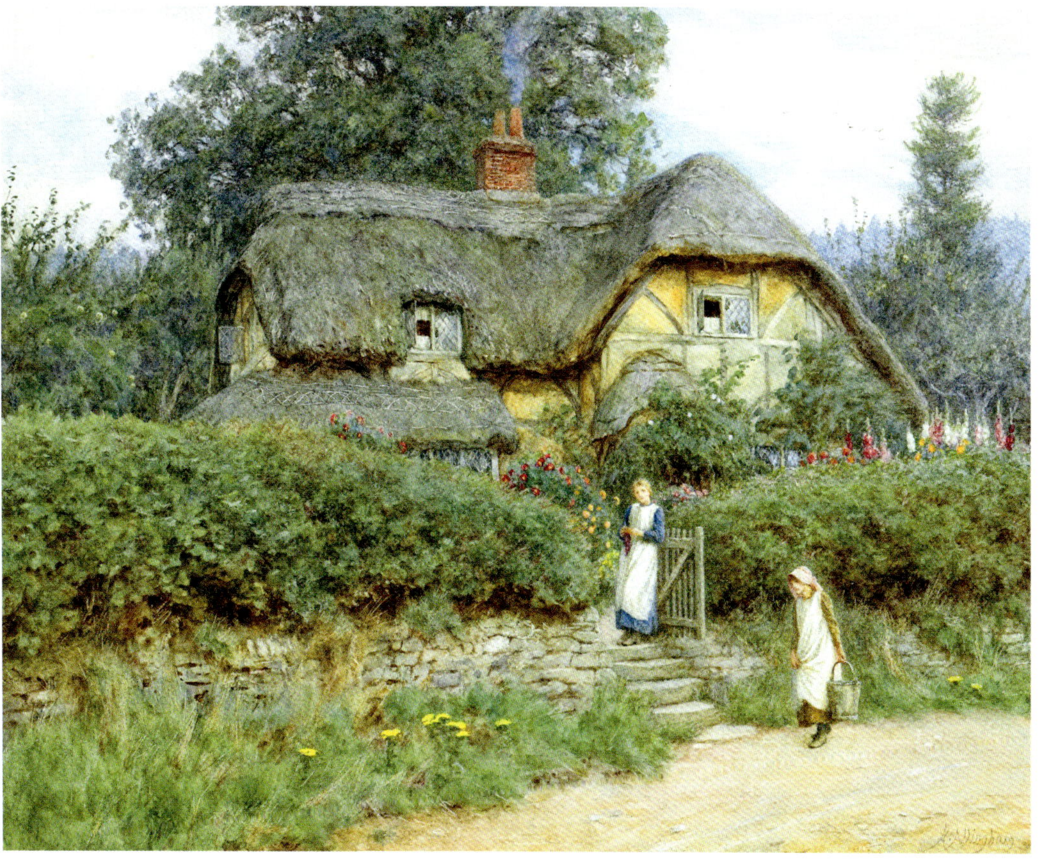

Although Jekyll is known today as a gardener she began her career as a painter, training at the South Kensington Schools, and exhibited briefly at the Royal Academy as well as copying works by J.M.W. Turner, including *The Fighting Temeraire* (1838, National Gallery, London) and *The Sun of Venice going to Sea* (1843, Tate).[5] Although Jekyll apparently abandoned painting because of myopia, it was through her study of artists such as Turner that she formed an interest in colour, notably the chromatic theories of the French chemist Michel Eugène Chevreul. Indeed, as Brent Elliott has noted, Jekyll's interest in colour theory, developed during her time as an art student, was paralleled by garden writers of the period.[6] From the 1870s, Jekyll's career as a writer and garden designer flourished, and her material success echoed in the large country house, Munstead Wood, designed for her in 1896 by Sir Edwin Lutyens. By the time of Spencer's boyhood, Jekyll was to garden design what Helen Allingham was to the painted garden – something of a national institution. As *The Times* noted in her obituary of 10 December 1932, Jekyll and her mentor, William Robinson, were credited with

> not only the complete transformation of English horticultural method and design, but also that wide diffusion of knowledge and taste which has made us almost a nation of gardeners. Miss Jekyll was also a true artist with an exquisite sense of colour.

In 1920 Edwin Lutyens commissioned a portrait of Jekyll from William Nicholson (National Portrait Gallery, London). Finding her a somewhat difficult sitter, Nicholson made a rather more distinguished painting of her gardening boots (Tate), which has acquired an iconic status reminiscent of the grand old lady of garden design herself.

As Stanley Spencer turned his attention increasingly towards the garden as a subject for his art during the 1930s, the combined legacy of Robinson, Jekyll, Parsons and Allingham was still a formidable presence, which had done much to define the relationship of the artist to the garden. Even so, the vision of "happy England" nurtured by such eminent figures in the visual culture of the garden remained resolutely elitist and upper class. Ties with the formality of the Victorian garden may have been loosened, and riots of colour were bursting forth in Jekyllian flower borders, but such confections were inalienably allied to a patrician garden culture. Here, on the one hand – at least in art and garden design – were carefully orchestrated 'wild' gardens tended by an army of invisible labourers; on the other were tumbledown cottages tenanted by the wives and children of the self-same labourers. The garden as depicted in later Victorian and Edwardian art was either an aesthetic retreat for the rich or a picturesque site for the elicitation of sympathy, inhabited by poor individuals who had no appreciation, or even awareness, of their picturesque circumstances. Certainly, as Keith Bell has observed, the success of Spencer's own garden paintings owed much to the continuing love affair of the upper middle classes with their green and pleasant land, appealing "to the readers of *Country Life*, with its idealized vision of solid rural English values".[7] Prominent among Spencer's patrons, notes Bell, were those who enjoyed the fruits of London-based business and the pleasures of the countryside, as well as aristocrats and wealthy expatriates. In that sense, Spencer's art represented a link to the conservative traditions of Parsons, Allingham and Jekyll. And yet, not everything in the garden was rosy.

For the majority of the population, whether in the town or in the country, the garden was not a timeless Elysium. Modern gardens included pocket-handkerchief-sized plots bounded by iron railings, ramshackle allotments with unruly vegetables and livestock, neatly ordered tulip beds in municipal parks, and banal hotel lawns. While the rural idyll was still pursued, and emerges in Spencer's own art, for example in *Cottages at Burghclere* (fig. 4), there was in existence a different and much more stimulating garden to behold in the not so happy England of the interwar period. Indeed, surveying Spencer's garden oeuvre from the mid 1920s to the late 1930s, one is struck by its diversity, and of course its magnificent quirkiness – the low brick wall and improvised rockery, juxtaposed with a goldfish tank in *Boatbuilder's Yard, Cookham* (fig. 15), the spindly sapling in its iron cage in *The Jubilee Tree, Cookham* (fig. 20), or the privet hedge and chimney pots

20
STANLEY SPENCER
The Jubilee Tree, Cookham, 1936
Oil on canvas, 91.4 x 75.6 cm
Art Gallery of Ontario, Toronto

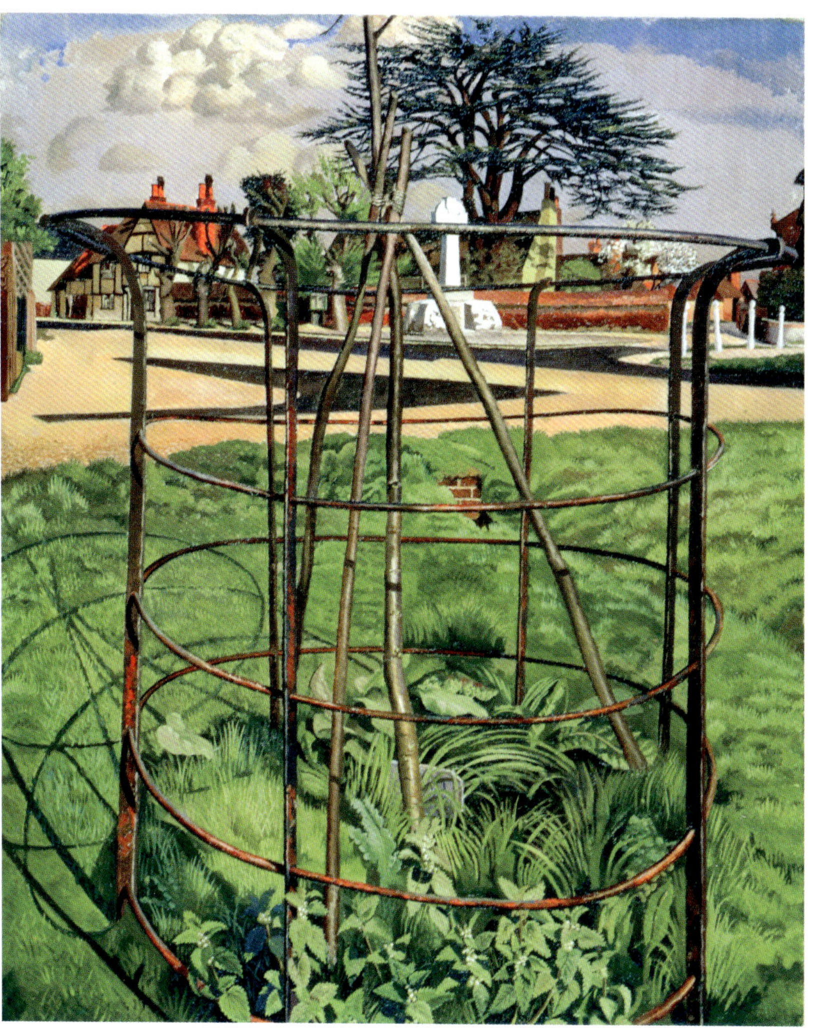

which provide the slightly incongruous context for *Wisteria, Cookham* (fig. 21). At times, Spencer casts his eye through the boundary of the garden to the landscape beyond, over fields and barbed-wire fences into urban streets and outbuildings. As motifs he often eschewed the appealing cottage in favour of something less alluring, such as *The Red House, Wangford* of 1926 (fig. 13) or *Cookham Rise* of 1938 (fig. 39). Whereas the former painting focuses on a stark red-brick, pantiled house, its pokey garden and line of washing forming a contrast to the surrounding fields and hayricks, the latter depicts a row of brand-new council houses on the outskirts of Cookham, each with a brand-new garden shed and a garden boundary marked out with concrete posts. Yet, as anyone who has travelled through Suffolk or Berkshire would know, Spencer's pictures are as representative of the reality of rural life in twentieth-century England as the thatched cottage.

Spencer continually bemoaned the fact that painting flowers, gardens and landscapes failed to provide him with the artistic or spiritual stimulation of his

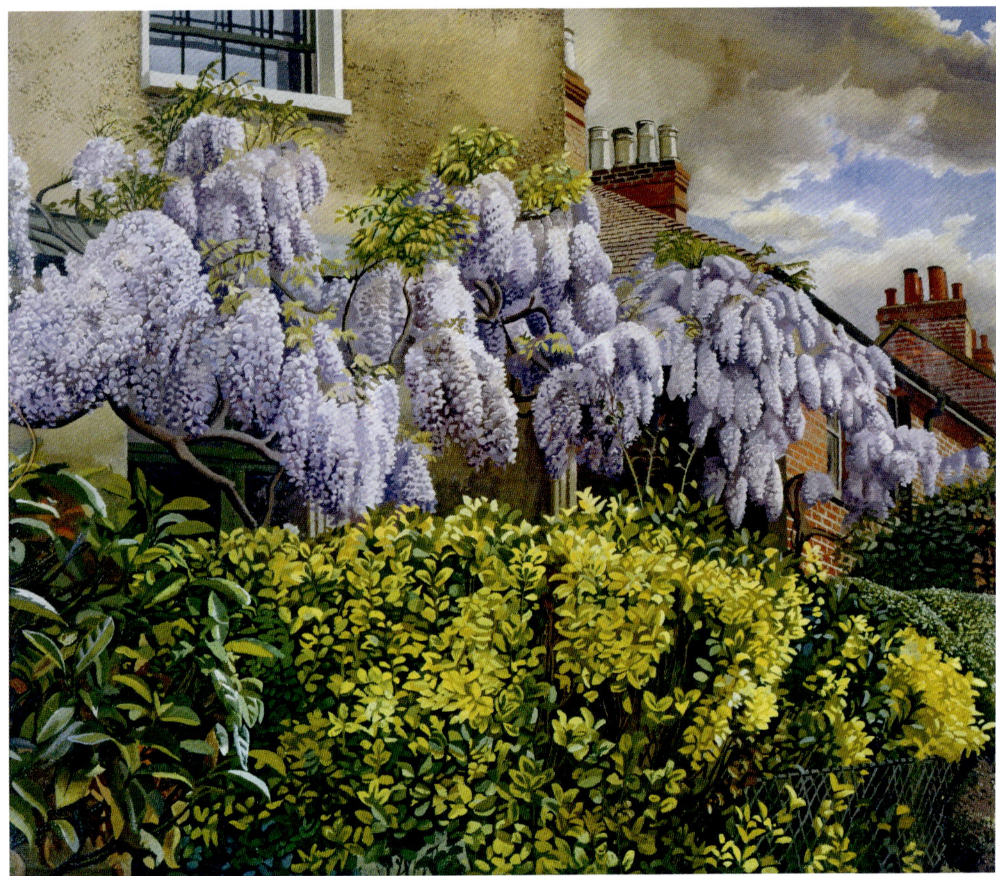

21
STANLEY SPENCER
Wisteria, Cookham, 1942
Oil on canvas, 63.5 x 76.2 cm
Harris Museum and Art Gallery, Preston

figurative works. Indeed the fact that he made them primarily as a response to commercial pressures supports his assertion that he was often unengaged by his subject-matter. Nonetheless, there was a type of garden that was perhaps peculiarly suited to Spencer's personality and gifts – the allotment. As a subject for art, the allotment had limited appeal to artists before the twentieth century, although since the 1790s it had been an important fixture in the rural economy, as labourers were provided with cottage gardens in order to alleviate their poverty. By the mid nineteenth century, allotment gardens were widespread, particularly in the south and west of England. In 1843 the Prime Minister, Sir Robert Peel, affirmed the importance of "small allotments" for leisure as well as sustenance.[8] As Jeremy Burchardt has argued, the allotment was allied to a progressive, liberal social policy, encouraging "respectability, independence, self-help and mutuality".[9] By the late nineteenth century allotments, which had originally been a rural phenomenon, had become widespread. With the migration of the rural population to towns and cities, railway and mining companies took the lead in the provision of allotment gardens, and in 1918 the National Union of Allotment Holders was established. While Spencer was probably oblivious to such developments, the ubiquity of the allotment garden in villages and towns had a marked impact on the country's gardenscape.

The original purpose and principal *raison d'etre* of the allotment was the cultivation of food. Thus it existed beyond the parameters of traditional garden aesthetics, its make-do-and-mend philosophy effectively undermining the tenets of imposed garden design. Spencer, as his allegorical paintings of dustmen, rubbish bins and litter indicate, revelled in detritus and disorder, enjoying the earthiness of the unkempt. It is not surprising, therefore, that his acknowledgement of allotment culture and its various associations emerges in some of his most engaging garden pictures, notably *Greenhouse and Garden* of 1937 (figs. 7, 9) in which a string of copper-skinned onions hangs prominently by a greenhouse door, or the spectacular *Goose Run, Cookham Rise* (1949, private collection), which takes as its unlikely subject a shambolic bird pen, littered with rotting vegetables, broken planks and wood shavings. Indeed, in Spencer's postwar garden paintings, of the later 1940s and into the 1950s, there is an increasingly subversive streak, and towards the end of his career he produced two works which, given the circumstances surrounding their commission, gave surprising prominence to the more down-to-earth aspects of garden culture. In 1951 he painted *Merville Garden Village near Belfast* (fig. 17), where his elder brother, Harold, then lived. While the picture included the recent modernist housing development by the architect Edward Prentice Mawson, Spencer's attention was drawn instinctively towards the dilapidated nursery with broken greenhouses and a corrugated-steel Nissen hut, situated incongruously in the middle of this new development. Similarly, in 1955, Spencer was commissioned by Plymouth City Council to celebrate the spirit of postwar reconstruction following extensive bomb damage during the Second World War. Instead, Spencer turned to the rather shabby nursery garden on Plymouth Hoe, with its peeling wooden cold frames and assorted bedding plants. As Robert Bartram has observed, Spencer's picture did allude, albeit obliquely, to Plymouth's resurgence and to local and national pride, with its inclusion of the Drake Monument on the Hoe as well as of the flowers destined for Plymouth's municipal gardens.[10] Even so, Spencer's idiosyncratic garden aesthetic was out of step with the times. By the end of the 1960s the government was determined to sanitize English allotment culture: a report commissioned in 1969 by the Ministry of Natural Resources insisted that the allotment holder would in future "no longer be able to cover his rhubarb with rusty old enamel buckets or protect his cucumbers with an old window frame propped up upon a heap of bricks".[11] Had Spencer still been alive he would surely have relished the subject the Ministry had so dismissively described.

Despite the attraction of gardens that many people would have regarded as eyesores, Stanley Spencer could appreciate more conventional forms of beauty. As a painter of flora he was highly responsive to the qualities of particular specimens, whether it was a laburnum or magnolia tree in full bloom (fig. 22),

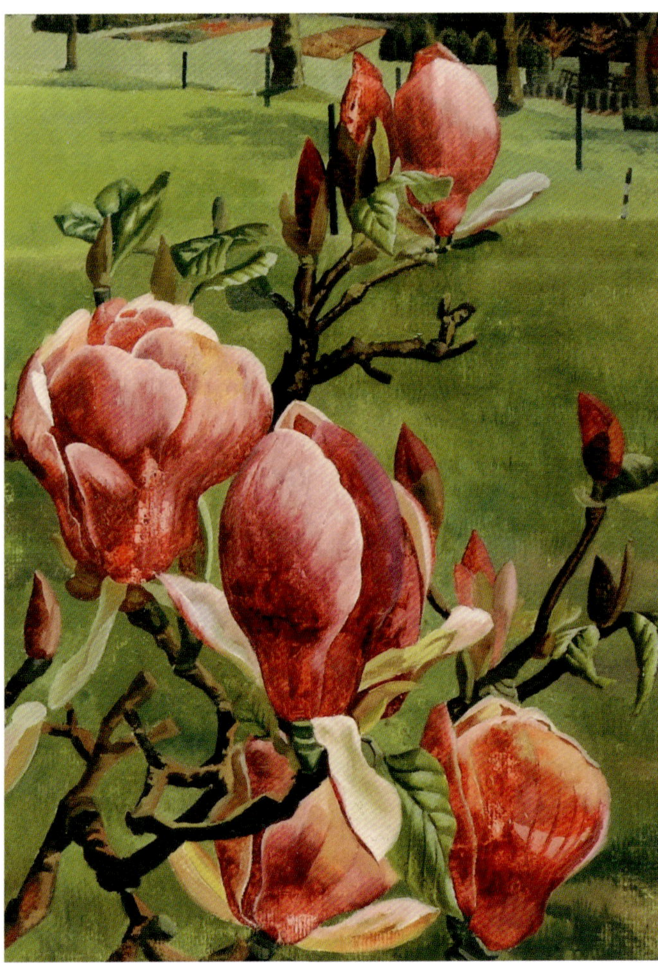

22
STANLEY SPENCER
Red Magnolia, 1938
Oil on canvas, 44.7 x 34.3 cm
Tullie House, Carlisle

potted geraniums, columbines, crocuses, poppies, peonies, gypsophila, or even the occasional exotic orchid. He was also sensitive to garden planting and design, as seen in his painting of the undulating rock garden at Cookham Dene (fig. 23). Even so, Spencer was not by inclination a horny-handed son of the soil, and while he painted flowers and gardens he had little personal interest in the garden other than as a motif for his art. However, at the time when Spencer began to take an interest in garden subjects for pragmatic reasons, a number of his contemporaries formed a serious interest in horticulture, which they allied to their artistic interests. Foremost among these was John Nash. Educated at Wellington College, Nash's early artistic development was influenced by his elder brother, Paul. Like many artists of his generation he served in the British army during the First World War, both as a soldier and as an official war artist. Nash had formed an interest in gardening at his parent's large country house in Buckinghamshire while still a child, but it was not until after the war that he began to explore horticultural subjects in earnest. As John Rothenstein later remarked, "Where Paul would write a manifesto or form a group, John transplanted some roses; where Paul would cherish the words of Thomas Browne or Blake, John consulted a seed catalogue".[12]

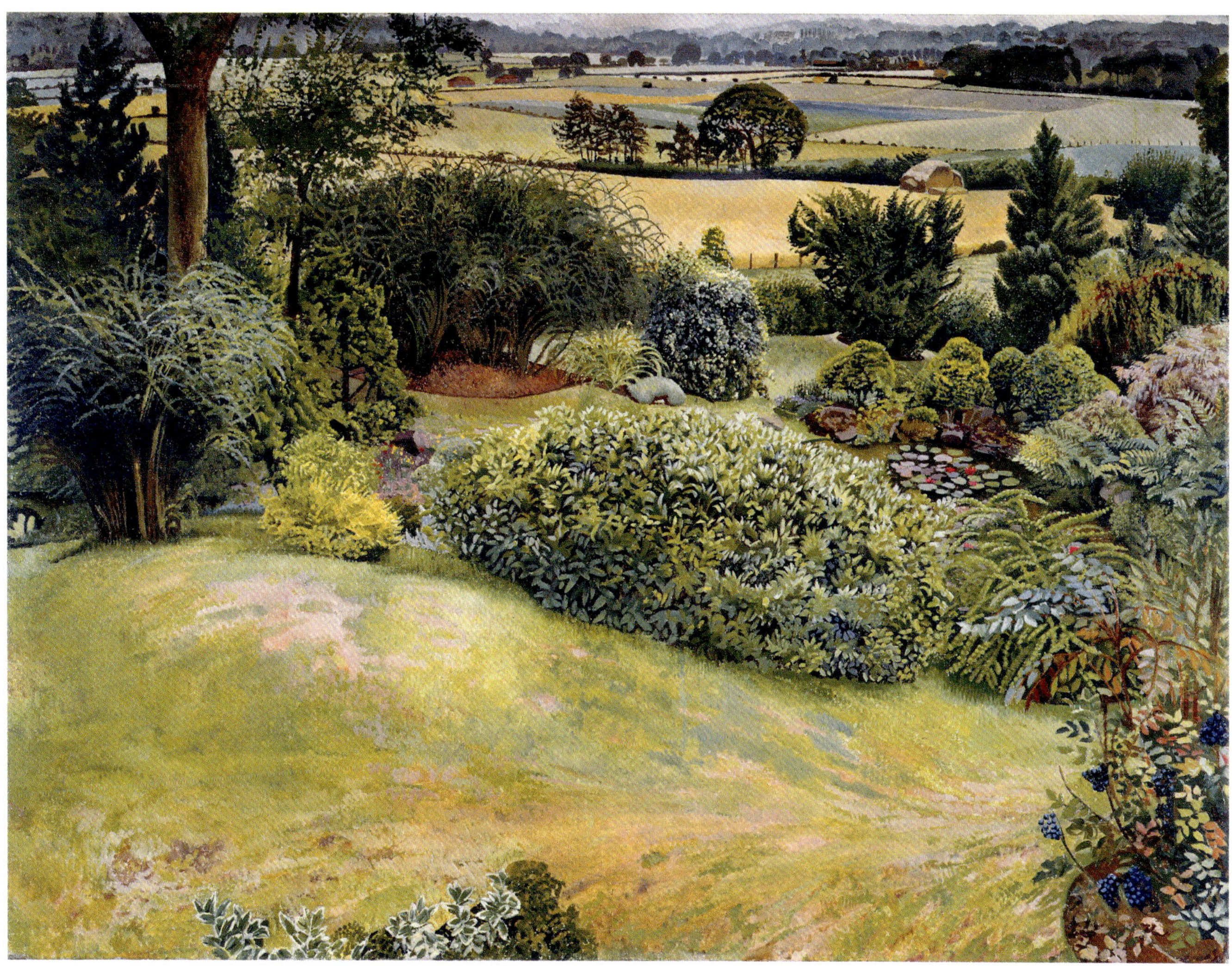

23
STANLEY SPENCER
Rock Garden, Cookham Dene, 1942
Oil on canvas, 71 × 94 cm
Birmingham Museum and Art Gallery

During the 1920s John Nash and his brother Paul were closely associated with the artists Richard and Sydney Carline and their sister Hilda, whose family home at 47 Downshire Hill, Hampstead, became a focal point for young painters – including Gilbert and Stanley Spencer – and in 1925 Stanley was to marry Hilda Carline. Although landscape was a shared interest for this group, and it doubtless did much to stimulate Spencer's own interest in the subject, for John Nash, with his absorption in botany and gardening, it was a passion. During the 1920s Nash, a talented wood engraver, began to produce illustrations for gardening books (fig. 24). They included William Dallimore's *Poisonous Plants* of 1927, *The Curious Gardener* of 1932 by Anthony Hampton (written under the pseudonym of Jason Hill), and *Flowers and Faces* of 1935, by the novelist and gardener H.E. Bates. In each case, the books were collaborations between the artist and writer, based upon friendship and mutual respect.

For John Nash, his commitment to horticulture necessitated close and continual contact with the countryside. In 1921 he moved to a cottage in Meadle,

24
JOHN NASH
Marrow and other Autumn Fruit and Flowers, 1935
Wood engraving on paper, 113.5 x 19.5 cm

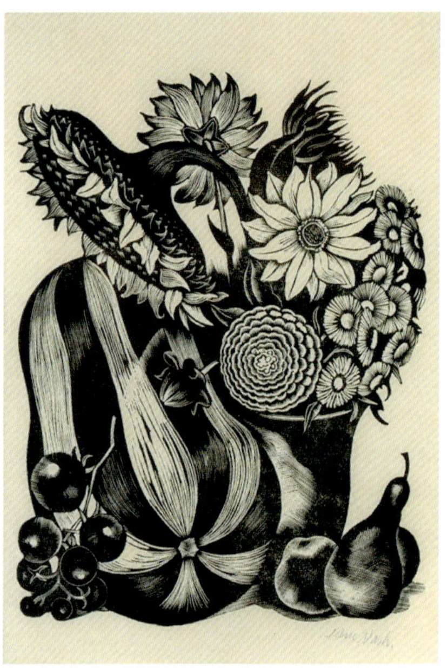

near Princes Risborough in Buckinghamshire, where he lived until 1944, when he established himself at Bottengoms Farm, Wormingfold, in Essex. For artist-gardeners like Nash, a sense of place and belonging was crucial to their art. During the interwar years a number of painters moved to the English countryside, using their specific location as a stimulus for their art and as a focal point for a wider artistic community. Prominent among these was Cedric Morris. Two years older than Spencer, Morris was, like John Nash, an ardent plantsman. Yet unlike Spencer or Nash, Morris had as a young man pursued an international career – working in Paris, where he associated with the artists Fernand Leger, Marcel Duchamp and Juan Gris, as well as with the expatriate American novelist Ernest Hemingway. Morris also travelled through Europe with his partner, Arthur Lett-Haines. During the 1920s Morris was active in London's avant-garde art scene, forming friendships with Ben Nicholson and Christopher Wood, and gaining membership of the Seven and Five Society. Given Morris's cosmopolitan circle, it seems all the more surprising that in 1929 he turned his back on London, moving with Lett-Haines to Pound Farm at Higham in Suffolk. It was here that Morris's passion for gardening was ignited. Inspired by Monet's garden at Giverny, Morris created, in the words of one of his students, "a paradise", interspersing plants and flowers with sculptures and reliefs by Lett-Haines and John Skeaping.[13] Gregarious by nature, Morris invited friends and colleagues to share his home and garden, establishing in 1937 the East Anglian School of Painting and Drawing at nearby Dedham, in the heart of 'Constable Country'. While the setting for the school lay in deepest rural Suffolk, Morris's curriculum was anything but conservative, allowing students to develop their own style and approach, reminiscent of contemporary French academic teaching. (Among the students who benefited from the liberal regime was the seventeen-year-old Lucian Freud, a student there in 1939.) Following a fire at the school, Morris and Lett-Haines relocated their home and the teaching to Benton End, a sixteenth-century house near Hadleigh, Suffolk. Here, Morris increasingly turned his attention towards horticulture, importing species from the Mediterranean and North Africa, and becoming, himself, an expert iris breeder (fig. 25). As well as artists, including John Nash, Duncan Grant and even Francis Bacon (not otherwise known for his love of the countryside), Morris's garden attracted prominent gardeners, notably Beth Chatto and Constance Spry.

Beth Chatto paid tribute to Cedric Morris when she described him as a "dirty hands gardener".[14] Indeed, it was this willingness among artists of Spencer's generation to combine their art with hands-on gardening that distinguished them from previous generations. Two young artists – less well known than either Morris or Nash – epitomized the spirit of "dirty hands" gardening during the 1930s, Charles Mahoney and Evelyn Dunbar, who combined their passion for art

25
CEDRIC MORRIS
Irises and Tulips, 1951
Oil on canvas, 109.2 x 83.8 cm
The New Art Gallery, Walsall

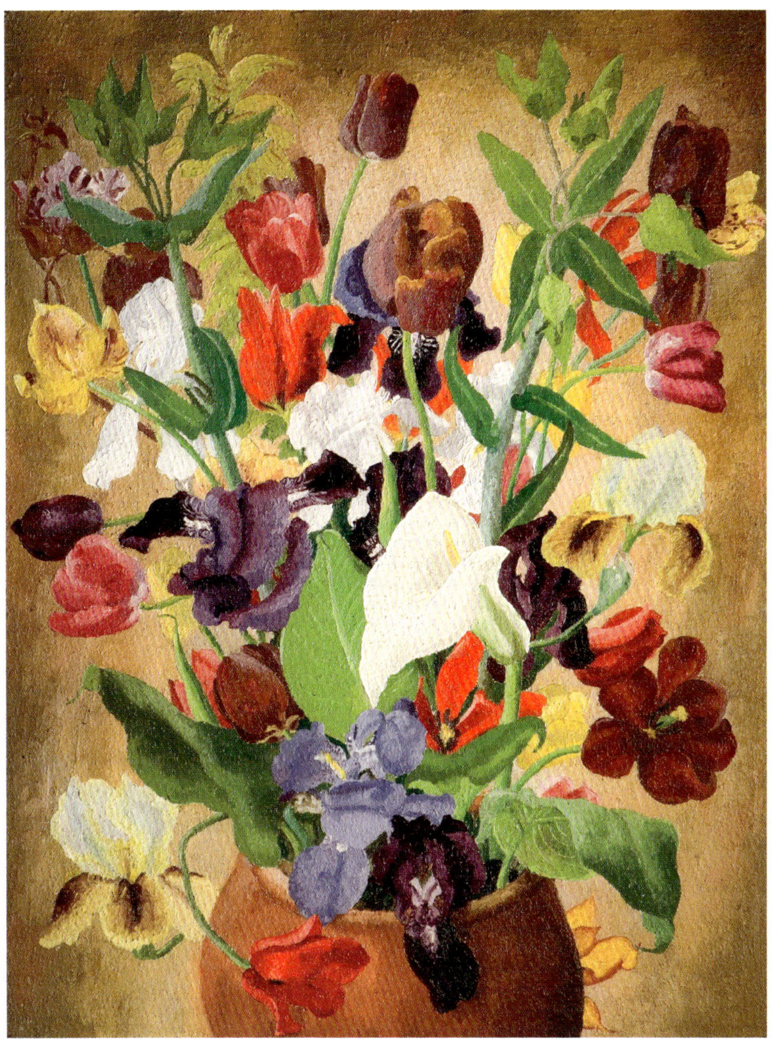

and gardening with an intense platonic love for one another, and, in Mahoney's case, with a strong adherence to socialist principles. Charles Mahoney was born in Lambeth, the son of a mechanical engineer. Baptized Cyril (but rechristened 'Charlie' by his artist friend Barnett Freedman), Mahoney lost an eye during a childhood accident, at the same time suffering a near fatal bout of diphtheria, making his subsequent achievements all the more remarkable.[15] Having gained a scholarship at the Royal College of Art in 1922, Mahoney subsequently joined the teaching staff, where he formed an interest in mural art and design. It was there, while working on a mural scheme at Brockley County School in 1933, that Mahoney formed an attachment to the RCA student Evelyn Dunbar.[16] Today Dunbar is known principally as a leading war artist, notably for her portrayals of land girls in the Woman's Land Army.[17] However, even before the war she had already developed an interest in the countryside through her passion for gardening. Unlike Mahoney, who constantly struggled with penury in his early years, Dunbar came from a prosperous middle-class background. At her parents' home, The Cedars at Strood, near Rochester in Kent, Dunbar established a studio, the 'Tower', adjacent to their extensive garden. Here Dunbar honed her gardening as well as her artistic skills, planting, cultivating and painting. At the same time, her horticultural interests drew Dunbar closer to Mahoney. One of the results of their friendship was a correspondence – of which, sadly, only Dunbar's letters survive, Mahoney's letters to Dunbar having been destroyed through parental pressure.[18] In the surviving letters Dunbar discussed visits to Kew Gardens and the Royal Horticultural Society shows at Vincent Square, often illustrating them with drawings, one of which is inscribed, "special vegetable garden, designed by Evelyn Dunbar, for the young man who would be most likely to appreciate it".[19] Mahoney and Dunbar, however, shared more than a common interest in gardening. As John Rothenstein observed in 1936, they had a "clear affinity of vision", stating that "Mr. Mahoney's influence upon her, has, I should judge, had an inspiring rather than a repressive effect, inasmuch as it has revealed to her certain elements latent in herself which, without it, she might have taken long to discover".[20] Among the fruits of this horticulturally oriented friendship was a book entitled *Gardeners' Choice*, published by Routledge in 1937. Unusually for such a volume, both text and images were by the artists themselves, supplemented by illustrations and descriptions of forty favourite plants, tail-pieces, and advice on designing and planting a garden. It was at this time that Mahoney acquired his first house and garden, the pretty sixteenth-century half-timbered Oak Cottage in the village of Wrotham, Kent. A decent plot of land surrounded the house and, after the war, Mahoney constructed a studio there from munitions packing cases. For the remainder of his life, Oak Cottage became the focus of Mahoney's artistic and family life, as he produced evocative studies of the garden and its varied plants.

While Mahoney and Stanley Spencer shared a common interest in the close observation of plants and flowers, the aspects of Mahoney's garden-inspired art that brought him most close in spirit to Spencer were his allegorical paintings. In 1928 Mahoney was chosen, with Edward Bawden and Eric Ravilious, to design a mural for the refectory at Morley College, London. Mahoney's contribution was *The Pleasures of Life* (1928–30), in which allegorical figures of the Muses, together with contemporary figures, were portrayed in an idyllic garden setting. Opened by the Prime Minister, Stanley Baldwin, it was unfortunately destroyed in 1940. Other allegorical works, aside from the Brockley murals, included *Adam and Eve* (1936), which Mahoney referred to in his correspondence with Evelyn Dunbar as "Charlie and Eve", and in which he could incorporate his passion for the garden and, presumably, his relationship with Dunbar.[21] In 1941 Mahoney was commissioned to paint a set of murals for Lutyens's Lady Chapel at Campion Hall,

Oxford, a scheme which preoccupied him until the early 1950s. Initially, Stanley Spencer had been chosen to paint the murals, and when he was eventually rejected (having proposed, for example, that he wished to use his mistress as the model for the Madonna) Mahoney took his place, at the suggestion of John Rothenstein. According to Rothenstein, Mahoney's murals for Campion Hall were second only "to that by Stanley Spencer at Burghclere".[22] Whether such an assessment was flattering to Mahoney, the comparison was surely a valid one, for, in his mural painting, often through the medium of the garden, Mahoney established a spiritual quality in his art which, like Spencer's, tapped into the wellspring of English romanticism.

Mahoney's artistic circle may have been less elevated than that of either Spencer or Cedric Morris, although he was, through his involvement with the Royal College of Art, aware of developments in the mainstream and avant-garde movements in British art. Among his artistic peers, however, Mahoney was closest to those who shared his passion for gardening, notably Edward Bawden, whom he had known as a student at the Royal College of Art. Edward Bawden, who, like the Nash brothers, came from a well-off background, worked in the 1920s as a professional illustrator and graphic artist, producing commercial images for London Transport and Westminster Bank, among others. And, as noted above, he had worked alongside Mahoney and Ravilious on the murals for Morley College. Yet although Bawden continued to pursue a career in the capital, in 1932 he moved to an imposing Georgian townhouse in the village of Great Bardfield in Essex, purchased for him by his father as a wedding present. As early as 1930 Bawden had corresponded with several artist friends, including Mahoney, Percy Horton and Geoffrey Rhoades, about setting up an artists' colony in the north-west Essex countryside. In the event, Bawden's artistic circle gravitated towards Great Bardfield – notably Eric Ravilious, who lived at Brick House from time to time; Michael Rothenstein; Mahoney himself; Evelyn Dunbar; and Geoffrey Rhodes, who helped Bawden decorate his new abode. Also attracted to Great Bardfield at this time was the landscape and figure painter John Aldridge, who acquired his own residence and who went into business with Bawden producing wallpaper designs. Aldridge, too, was an avid gardener, and, as with Mahoney and Morris, his own garden at Place House, as well as the countryside around Great Bardfield, formed one of the central motifs of his work (fig. 26). It was also Aldridge who, in the years following the Second World War, established Great Bardfield – for better or for worse – as a fashionable artists' colony along the lines of Newlyn and St Ives, organizing popular 'open house' summer exhibitions and attracting hordes of tourists, as well as artists, to this corner of north-west Essex.

In many ways, the 1930s saw an unparalleled growth of interest among English artists in the garden, not merely as a subject but as an object in its own

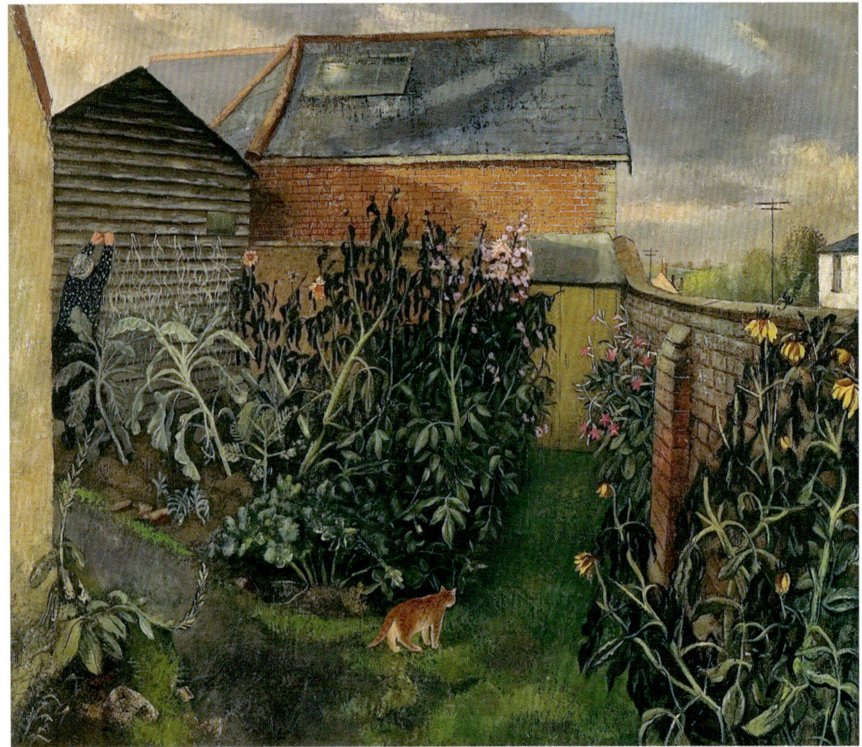

26
JOHN ALDRIDGE
First Frost, 1950s
Oil on canvas, 63.5 x 76 cm
Royal West of England Academy, Bristol

right. Artists such as John Nash, Cedric Morris, Charles Mahoney and Evelyn Dunbar were in the forefront of this movement, fostering not only an interest in plants and gardens among artists, but also a community of artist gardeners. With the outbreak of the Second World War this community, like many others, was shattered. Artists continued to paint gardens, but the idyll of "happy England" was never quite the same. Among those painters who captured the impact of the war upon the hitherto Edenic garden was Eliot Hodgkin, who, during his breaks as an air-raid warden in London, used his skills as a botanical painter to capture the impromptu gardens which sprang up from seeds self-sown among the ruins created by the Blitz. For, as the botanist J. Edward Lousley observed at the time: "If the streets of London in 1944 and 1945 were not paved with gold it may at least be said that the bombed sites were clothed with the golden flowers of a Ragwort from Mount Etna and the silver of a Fleabane from Canada!"[23] In the postwar period the English countryside remained a haven for artists, but by the 1950s it was also a refuge. One such artist was Spencer's contemporary Ivon Hitchens. And yet, while Hitchens was only two years younger than Spencer, his art was light years away. Hitchens had for decades painted the English countryside, having a particular affection for the Sussex Downs and Shropshire. In 1940 Hitchens's Hampstead studio was bomb-blasted. With his wife and child, he escaped to West Sussex, where on Lavington Common he pitched his caravan in a dense thicket, without water or electricity. Gradually, he established a house among the woods (Greenleaves), and a garden of sorts, which he used as a source of inspiration for his art (fig. 27). As Ben Tufnell has observed, Hitchens's art was not concerned at all with the 'spirit of the place', symbolism, or with conventional garden aesthetics. Rather, he used the garden and the surrounding woodland to explore form, depth and space.[24] For Hitchens his wild, secluded garden provided an environment in which he could solve pictorial problems. His garden may not have been aesthetically attractive, nor did he refer to it pictorially in a conventional manner. However, in the privacy it offered it served as a *hortus conclusus*, and, as has been observed, Hitchens's isolation in his Sussex garden, "from being a wartime necessity, became a habit and then a personal need".[25] Like John Nash, Mahoney and Morris, Hitchens was drawn compulsively to the garden. And as he trundled his wheelbarrow, laden with canvases, paints, brushes, groundsheets and umbrella, around his damp, six-acre Sussex woodland wilderness, Hitchens – like Spencer, pushing his pram perennially through the streets of Cookham – was on a similar journey of self-discovery, cultivating the garden of the mind.

27
IVON HITCHENS
Damp Autumn, 1941
Oil on canvas, 40.6 x 74.3 cm
Tate

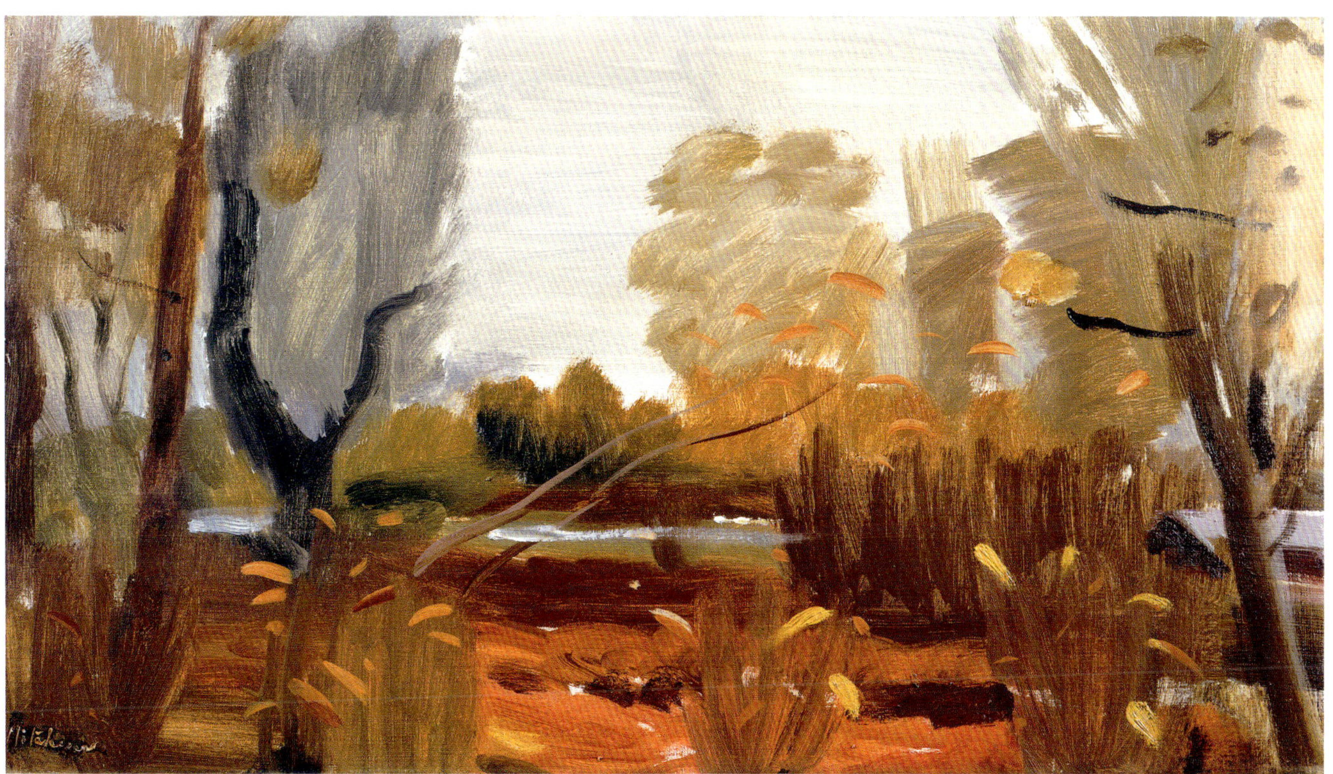

HOMES & GARDENS

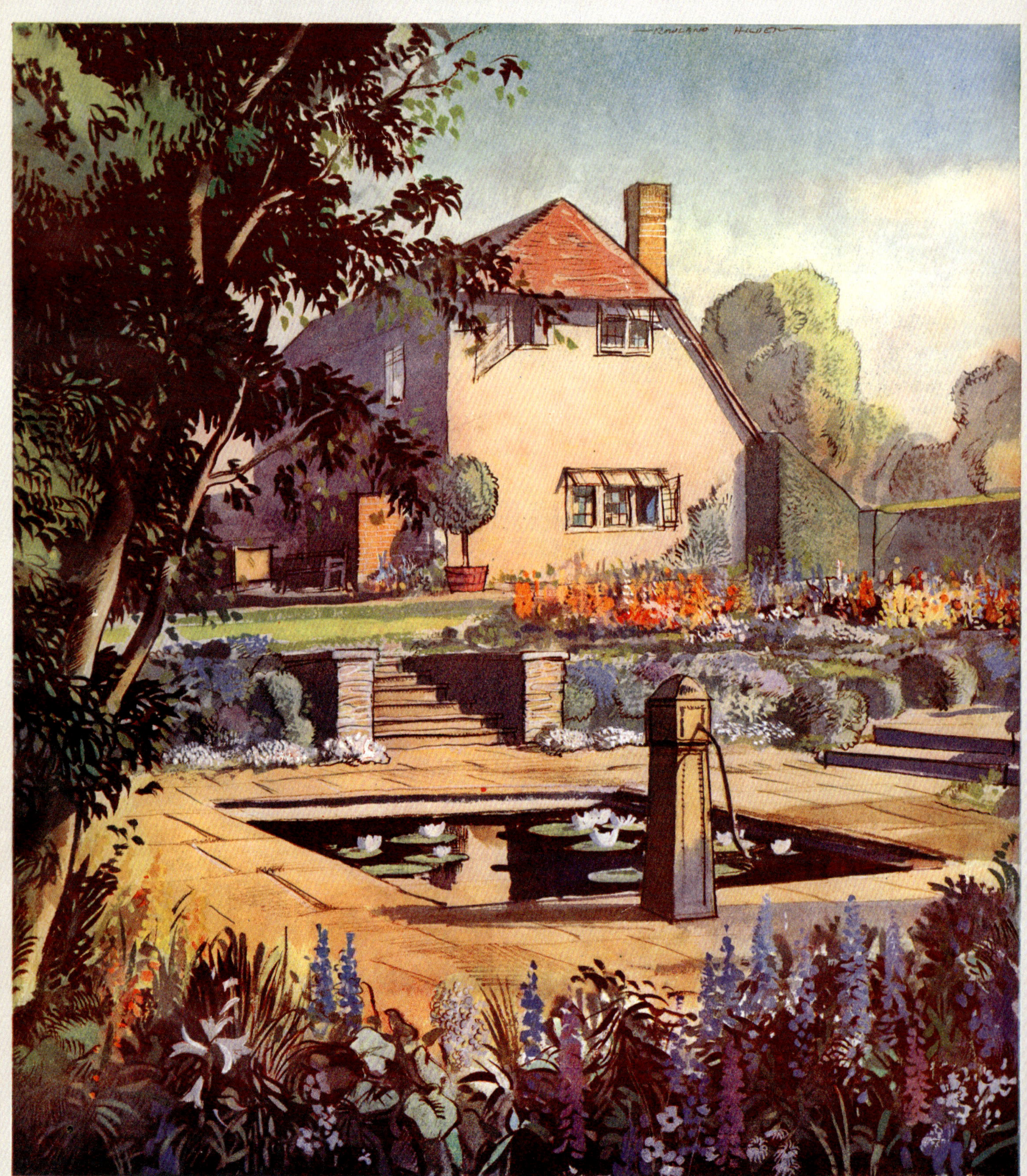

JULY, 1939

SMALL POOLS FOR THE GARDEN

ONE SHILLING

LANDSCAPES AND GARDENS OF THE LONG WEEKEND

Jeremy Gould

Over four million houses were built in the "Long Weekend", the apt title given by Robert Graves and Alan Hodge to the period between 1918 and 1939.[1] This represented about one third of the housing stock of Britain; indeed, the rate of house building per year – 200,000 in the depression years of the 1920s, and 350,000 houses in 1936 alone – has never been equalled. About three quarters of these houses were constructed for private owners and were for sale – mortgage borrowing rose from £66 million in 1914 to £700 million by 1939 – and the remainder were built by local authorities as council housing for rent under the various Housing Acts that followed the Tudor Walters Report of 1918.[2] Almost all were one- and two-storey detached or semi-detached houses, or in short terraces. Flats, whether privately or local authority-owned, were a rarity, reserved for the inner city.

This spate of building represented a general drift in the population from the countryside to the cities and towns. Between 1918 and 1939 the population of London rose by some two million to 7,250,000. This total constituted one fifth of the population of England and Wales and one quarter of the nation's urban population. The 1931 census showed that over 80 per cent of people lived in areas that were classified as urban, prompting G.M. Young to declare that "we are the most urban nation in the world".[3] The building plots for the new suburbs came from agricultural land that happened to be adjacent to existing conurbations and some 66,200 acres were consumed annually.[4] The one feature held in common by all this housing was that every house had a garden.

Garden City gardens

The Tudor Walters Report influenced state and private housing standards for the next two decades and beyond. While Tudor Walters and his committee were mainly concerned with issues of layout, sanitation and floor areas, there were strong political motives in improving housing standards for the "poorer classes" (and troops returning from the First World War) to avoid the possibility of social unrest or Bolshevist revolution. Principal in its recommendations were that houses should have internal bathrooms and parlours (that is, a second living room); that all homes should be sited within planned layouts where housing densities should not exceed twelve houses per acre; and that back gardens should be a minimum of 400 square yards in size. Thus established middle-class standards should be applied to working-class housing.

28
Rowland Hilder, **'Small pools for the garden'**, front cover of *Homes & Gardens*, July 1939

> If there is one part of these proposals that appeals to me … it is that houses shall be provided in semi-rural conditions with good garden plots and with good transport access to the work in which the man is engaged, so that he can do his work in the factory while his family can live in fresh air under semi-rural conditions and in a properly constructed house and where, when he gets home at night, he will find not only a healthy family, but healthy occupation outside where they can go and work together in the garden.[5]

The provision of gardens as an agent of social reform was not new. It was a fundamental principle of Ebenezer Howard's 'Garden City' of 1902, which Frederick Osborn described as "much a city *in* a garden – that is surrounded by beautiful country – as a city *of* gardens".[6] Howard's housing plots were a minimum of 222 square yards and an average of 289 square yards. For social reformers of the early twentieth century, the activity of gardening was seen as healthy family exercise and an opportunity to grow vegetables, any surplus of which working-class families could sell to supplement their income. For Quaker reformers such as George Cadbury at Bournville (begun in 1895) and Joseph Rowntree at New Earswick (begun in 1901) there was the additional moral crusade to divert the working man from the public house and encourage him "back to the land".[7] The architect of New Earswick was Raymond Unwin, a member of the Tudor Walters committee and its major architectural influence. The New Earswick plot size of 350 square yards was "determined upon after careful consideration of the amount a man can easily and profitably work by spade cultivation in his leisure time".[8] Unwin used a simple Arts and Crafts architectural language for his terraces of houses set back from the streets with small front gardens and larger, private back gardens (fig. 29). The street scene was carefully composed of symmetrical and asymmetrical buildings, closed vistas and consistently detailed front walls, hedges and trees. Similar layouts were used at Letchworth, the first Garden City (built from 1903, with Adshead & Ramsey as architects), and Hampstead Garden Suburb (begun in 1906, by Unwin and others), while in 1909 Unwin published his *Town Planning in Practice*, which demonstrated his ideas and solutions to the creation of ideal suburbs. The physical result was a sort of *rus in urbe*, which had much in common with the bosky, affluent middle-class Victorian suburb, such as Norman Shaw's Bedford Park on the edge of West London (begun in 1877), and was both a potent symbol of Pooterish social position for the working classes (for whom the Tudor Walters Report was intended) and a model for middle-class speculative housing.

Gardens fit for heroes

Inevitably, working-class homes, built with government subsidies by local authorities following the Addison Act of 1919, were invariably plainer, although

29
Raymond Unwin, **Houses and gardens in New Earswick, York,** 1910
University of York
Borthwick Institute

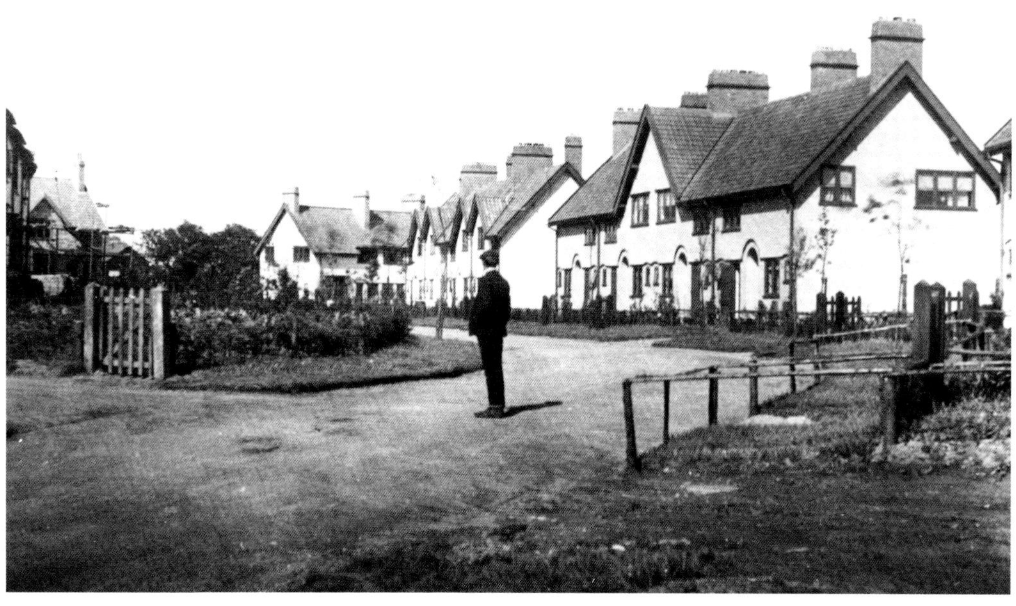

the opportunities for creating new gardens were similar and the plots often more generous in size. The greatest of these were the 'cottage' estates built on the fringes of London under the auspices of G. Topham Forrest, chief architect to the London County Council. The Becontree Estate in Dagenham (begun in 1921; fig. 30) consisted of 26,000 houses, and was home to 120,000 people; the Bellingham and Downham Estates south of Lewisham (built from 1921 and 1924 respectively) contained about 10,000 houses, and the St Helier Estate (1927), south of the new Morden underground station, comprised a modest 9,500 houses.[9] It would be wrong to assume that the new tenants, moved out from inner-city slums, did not possess the necessary gardening knowledge to till their newly given plots. There was an established practice of flower, vegetable and fruit growing from the nineteenth-century allotment tradition, and the intense cultivation of the urban backyard that this engendered could be transferred to the new suburbs.[10] The local authorities, however, controlled the road verges and other recreational spaces and, through Tenants' Handbooks, ensured that front gardens were kept "in a neat and cultivated condition".[11] Front gardens were not used for vegetable growing but for ebullient displays of multi-coloured bedding plants, representing the sole opportunity for personal expression, which was in turn encouraged by council-sponsored competitions. Councils were also responsible for trimming the ubiquitous privet hedges and for the sparse tree planting in the verges, which generally failed to relieve these somewhat dull and repetitive suburban areas.

The difference between the landscape of the 'Addison' estates and that of contemporary Welwyn Garden City could not have been more marked. The principle of establishing a new town "for healthy living and industry",[12] where "a man will have the time and energy after his work is done for leisure and recreation",[13] was sold as much on the quality of its lawns, trees and flower beds as on its respectable neo-Georgian red-brick architecture or the promise of local employment. Like Becontree, the Welwyn Garden City site was originally farmland (although it was, admittedly, hilly and wooded) but its layouts were less dense and more flexibly planned than those of its predecessors, and designed to incorporate as many existing trees and hedgerows as possible. Houses were developed more slowly (the population of Welwyn had only reached 8,586 by 1931 and 21,000 by 1941) and in small groups, so that at any one time it had the appearance of completeness. Its architect, Louis de Soissons, had overall control of all the buildings and landscaping, although many other architects and builders were involved. De Soissons had been trained at the École des Beaux-Arts in Paris, and the centre of Welwyn was formed from two great Beaux-Arts axial spaces – the appropriately named Howard's Way, creating an approach from the railway station, and the great Parkway, 200 feet wide and at right angles to Howard's Way. Parkway was planted with symmetrical avenues of pleached limes and white-beams, with formal beds of roses and other shrubs. The layout of the houses incorporated existing field oaks and elms, although some streets had more formal planting of Lombardy poplars intended to give the effect of church spires, "an essential upwards element in townscapes". Poplars were also used to 'camouflage' the rather ordinary brick-built factories in the industrial zone as well as providing

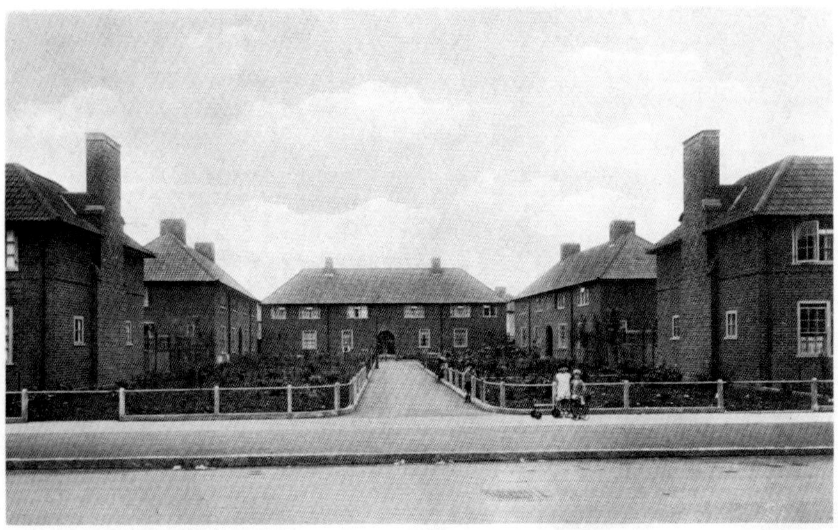

30
Becontree Estate, Essex
(from 1921), nos. 321–47 Hedgeman's Road, c.1930, from Montague H. Cox, *Housing 1928–30* (London County Council, 1931)

STANLEY SPENCER'S ARCHITECTURE

Steven Parissien

As Professor Keith Bell has noted in his essay, above, Stanley Spencer's garden pictures have, in the past, been largely overlooked by critics and biographers. Commentators have tended to follow both the condescending reception often afforded to them by critics at the time and pejorative remarks Spencer himself made towards the end of his life, when he appeared increasingly concerned that he should be remembered by posterity primarily for his religious works. Accordingly, at least until Keith Bell's catalogue raisonné of 1992,[1] these views have frequently been viewed as a necessarily moneymaking yet somewhat mundane prelude to the mystical religious masterpieces of Spencer's last decades. To critics of the 1930s, there seemed to be no cutting-edge, modernist agenda in such work, and no avant-garde technique. As Professor Bell has noted of these paintings: "Academic criticism has for the most part ignored the landscape paintings mainly, perhaps, because it was felt that any judgment of his achievement must be founded upon the works which the artist himself felt to be central to his career."[2] The fact that these works were also far more immediately accessible than Spencer's celebrated visionary subjects did not aid their critical reception.

Undoubtedly, the growing popularity of Spencer's local views, garden pictures and landscapes during the interwar years gave him a degree of unaccustomed financial stability. And certainly the pressure on him to earn enough money to maintain this fiscal equilibrium was heavy. However, the income from these pictures was not the primary reason for their creation. The subsequent derogatory judgements on Spencer's garden and landscape views indeed miss the point of these works. Many of them were explicitly designed to demonstrate the interrelationship between natural and man-made spaces and, perhaps more importantly, to communicate the artist's peculiarly personal view of heaven – a heaven which was revealed to him, and him alone, in the small, tightly defined gardens and overgrown backyards of his home village of Cookham in Berkshire.

Spencer himself was often prone to repudiate his garden pictures in public. In 1927 he complained that "no sort of spiritual activity comes into the business at all",[3] and in May 1933 he moaned to his long-suffering dealer, Dudley Tooth, that "As I feared, every one as usual wants my landscapes", declaring that "I am very sorry public galleries are taking my landscapes as representative works of mine".[4] Yet by 1935 he was so deeply in debt that he was exhorting Tooth to sell his landscapes for whatever they would fetch. And in 1938 – his most productive year for this genre – most of the nineteen still lifes and landscapes Spencer painted were quickly sold. Three years later, though, in a characteristic outburst of self-flagellation, he grumbled: "I am not pleased with myself over my landscape work, it never having been what I intended or wanted to do & having done them only to get money".[5]

36
STANLEY SPENCER
The Betrayal (detail), 1936
Oil on canvas, 123 x 137 cm
Ulster Museum and Art Gallery

However, it is always unwise (as a number of his early biographers did), to take Stanley Spencer's comments on his own works at face value.[6] By the end of his life he was particularly keen to distance himself from his garden and landscape views, preferring to direct critics to his more ostensibly visionary works. But in 1941 he acknowledged of his garden views that there "are those which have a definite emotion as their basis & on the strength of which the subject has been chosen", and that "All feelings of mine might be found in some measure in each".[7] Similarly, in July 1959, shortly before Spencer's death, John Rothenstein reported that, during a visit to his home, the artist had strenuously maintained that "The necessity for painting landscapes to ensure his survival ... had given him a positive antipathy for landscape" – and that, to underline this statement, he had "insisted throughout his visit upon sitting with his back to a window".[8] However, moments after making this declaration, Spencer completely contradicted himself, and calmly told Rothenstein that he would like to return to Oxfordshire soon to paint the River Thame at Newington.

It is unlikely that even the most accessible of Spencer's garden canvases were, in truth, wholly devoid of meaning and symbolism. As Keith Bell has noted, even the simplest fence and the subtlest bush could, through Spencer's eyes, be charged with a hidden, mystical significance. In the 1954 publication *Sermons by Artists*, Spencer admitted that, shortly after he had moved back to Cookham, "quite suddenly I became aware that everything was full of special meaning and this made everything holy".[9] Three years later he acknowledged that "Everything for me has (especially the visible world) a degree of meaning".[10]

Spencer's virtuoso treatments of the gardens and architecture of Cookham and its immediate surroundings are in fact crucial to any understanding of the artist's approach to life and art. He used these canvases as a way of explaining – through the prism of his undoubtedly eccentric personal vision – the increasingly tense interplay between the natural world and the built environment, and the allegories of paradise afforded by even the most mundane of gardens. His paintings demonstrate the artist's immense feeling for, and understanding of, the way in which English landscape and the traditional English garden were changing after the First World War, and how contemporary development was redefining and eradicating familiar streets and spaces. Spencer focused on the relationship between the home, the garden and the wider world. His spaces could be a tiny front area, with a few plants brutally circumscribed by masonry or gravel, or, alternatively, a less well ordered but nevertheless still vulnerable world of fields and hedgerows. But each one carries within it an element of potential change and a suggestion of higher significance.

The everyday architecture of the home and the street was central to Spencer's imagination. Narrow front areas, neglected back gardens and overgrown yards all sharply defined the parameters and content of his work, and provided the essential framework for his stories. Spencer's garden pictures are not only about the forms and colours of nature. He glories just as much in the English building tradition as in the bushes and flowers of Cookham's gardens, celebrating the warm, russet reds and the changing patinas of terracotta and brick as much as he does the natural exuberance of the adjacent vegetation. His garden pictures make a prominent feature of the architecture of everyday life, and he sites many of his views at the interface of brick walls and garden shrubberies. In these works, both the man-made and natural environments are trying to assert their precedence. Spencer's plants are more often than not imprisoned within a tight girdle of fences, walls or pots. The natural world is tamed, subjugated and organized; untrammelled nature is kept at a distance. He records the physical interaction of hard, inflexible surfaces and insinuating and adaptable plant life. The artist is actually delineating lines of battle, albeit that the encounters he describes are peculiarly subtle and well mannered.

Spencer's garden pictures were not merely representations of timeless English values, but also provided a gentle caution for the future. Yet in these works he was not making a judgement. He did not overtly side either with the conservationists and gardeners or with the developers and builders. He merely recorded the everyday altercations he saw in the manner of the war artist he had formerly been. Thus in his *Merville Garden Village near Belfast* of 1951 (fig. 17), the natural world of bushes, creepers and burgeoning undergrowth is dispassionately depicted overcoming the clumsily rendered wall in the foreground and the war-time huts and greenhouses beyond, while the new housing block sits mutely in the background, protected by a wall – calmly observing the battle from a safe distance, much in the same manner as Spencer himself viewed the everyday interplay of architecture and nature from behind his walls and fences.

The growing idealization of the garden and its broader landscape context of the interwar years – epitomized in the naively utopian, anti-capitalist and anti-socialist 'Distributist' or 'Back to the Land' movement of the 1920s and 1930s, and the new enthusiasm for outdoor activities such as hiking or cycling – is implied, if not overtly spelled out, in Spencer's works. In these years interest was increasing, too, in the notion of the 'English' garden, stimulated by the gardens of designers such as Gertrude Jekyll, whose innately English compositions, cleverly reinventing tradition for the twentieth century, were widely publicized in magazines such as *Country Life* and *The Garden*. According to Keith Bell, this revival of interest in historic gardens and plants "probably accounts for the popularity of Spencer's garden scenes, which were purchased by ardent gardeners like the Countess Cawdor".[11]

Spencer's celebration of Cookham's architecture also reflected the growing appreciation for the value of historic landscape and the historic built environment after 1918, and the belief that, as Alexandra Harris has noted, "it might be the humble village that offered the best model for the future of English life – that, as poet and writer Edmund Blunden proposed in 1941, villages such as Cookham might prove 'the salvation and fulfilment of England'".[12] Spencer's village views reflected a new interest between the wars in the concept – and future – of 'Englishness', as is evident from the success of books such as F.J. Harvey Darton's *English Fabric: A Study of Village Life* of 1935, H.J. Massingham's 1937 hiker's guide to English history, *The Genius of England*, John Betjeman's frequent BBC radio broadcasts on English village life, and the popular English Heritage series of books that Longman began to publish from 1929 (one of the first titles of which was Eric Parker's *English Wild Life*). As Jeremy Gould has noted elsewhere in this book, this growing interest in the role and value of the historic English village was also reflected in the rediscovery of works by that indefatigable chronicler of eighteenth-century Selborne, Gilbert White. As Alexandra Harris has observed, White's journals, edited by Walter Johnson, were published in 1931, and were constantly reissued with other commentaries during the ensuing decade. The 1935 edition of White's *Natural History of Selborne*, edited by W.T. Williams and G.H. Vallins, presented the original work "rather as a literary masterpiece than as a scientific treatise".[13] In 1938 *The Times Literary Supplement* went so far as to label Gilbert White "The Discoverer of England".[14]

One of the principal public battlegrounds for the growing conservation movement of the interwar years was very familiar to Spencer – Hampstead in North London. In the spring of 1914 the 6th Earl of Mansfield, owner of Kenwood House, began negotiations with a developer's syndicate, comprising a group of builders, with a view to developing the whole of the ancient estate, which covered much of Hampstead Heath. At the end of the war horrified locals made a number of offers for the estate, and in 1919 formed the Kenwood Preservation Committee (KPC). But despite an agreement of December 1921 to offer the house and estate to the KPC, the house's contents were sold at auction on 6 November 1922. The following month the KPC managed to buy 100 acres of the Heath, with the London County Council buying a further 32 acres in 1924. In 1925, however, a white knight in the form of the Guinness tycoon, Edward, 1st Earl of Iveagh, bought the remaining 74 acres, intending to leave the house and grounds to the nation on his death – which came after only two years.[15] (A similar tale had already unfolded at the Marble Hill estate by the River Thames at Twickenham. In 1901 the Trustees of the Peel estate sold the whole area to developers, and machinery was already in place to begin the work when the London County Council offered half of the £70,000 they had paid, and other local authorities made up the rest.[16] Today both Marble Hill and Kenwood are, thankfully, in the care of the government agency English Heritage.)

Spencer cannot have been unaware of Hampstead Heath's plight. His first wife's family, the Carlines, lived at 47 Downshire Hill, not far from the Heath, and he was often invited there. Spencer could not fail to be aware – as was the rest of the nation – that the Heath was now in peril of development. And if Spencer could not save Hampstead, he could try and hold back the pace of development in Cookham itself. In 1931 he wrote of the village that "It is nonsense to think of Cookham as being a sort of Maidenhead or Taplow or Bourne End. As long as the rites of the commons does not become changed it can never be more than one street surrounded by green fields, commons, scores of footpaths, & hills."[17] Spencer's view of the restriction and erosion of nature was shared by many Britons in the interwar years. The two decades after 1918 saw a substantial increase in awareness of what Britain was losing in terms of its historic rural and built environments. The Society for the Preservation of Ancient Buildings (SPAB) and the National Trust had already been founded, in 1877 and 1895 respectively. (In 1929 the SPAB co-published its invaluable guide to the treatment of historic homes, A.R. Powys's *The Repair of Ancient Buildings*.) To these were now added the Council for the Care of Churches, in 1921; the Ancient Monuments Society, in 1924; the Council for the Preservation of Rural England, in 1926; and the Georgian Group, founded as an offshoot of the SPAB in 1935. In 1932 local authority Preservation Orders were introduced, although Britain had to wait until 1948 for the full-blooded protection of old buildings in the form of listing or, as it is now termed, designation.

Of all these bodies, the CPRE was perhaps most akin to Spencer's view of England. In 1926 the planner Sir Patrick Abercrombie published a book entitled *The Preservation of Rural England*, in which he called for a national committee to preserve the countryside. This was duly formed in December 1926 as the Council for the Preservation of Rural England (CPRE), with Abercrombie as its Honorary Secretary. The CPRE's first campaigns were attacks on ribbon development, which were ultimately rewarded with the passing of the Restriction of Ribbon Development Act in 1935. From 1928 CPRE Architectural Advisory Panels were set up jointly with the Royal Institute of British Architects to advise local authorities and developers on good quality design for new buildings. In 1930 CPRE proposed an "open belt" of protected countryside around London, and three years later publicly endorsed Raymond Unwin's recommendation of a "Green Girdle" for London, which was to become Britain's first green belt in the postwar years.

Jeremy Gould evaluates the importance and influence of the newborn CPRE elsewhere in this book. However, it is worth noting in this context that one of the paeans published in praise of this new pressure group appears particularly to reflect Spencer's village-centred philosophy. In 1928 the youthful CPRE was eulogized in a polemic which soon became a national bestseller, *England and the Octopus*, written by the then unknown young architect Clough Williams-Ellis. The book condemned many of the developments which were subtly delineated in Spencer's interwar paintings: the "spate of mean building ... that is shrivelling up old England". "England is being rapidly disfigured," declared Williams-Ellis; "We saved our country [in the war] that we might destroy it". Like Spencer in *Cookham Rise*, he celebrated the high standard of contemporary local authority housing: "had there been no new housing but Council housing since the War we had been in far happier case to-day, so far as the look of England is concerned". Like Spencer, too, he sought everyday buildings which "should be congruous with their settings, suitable to and harmonious in their surroundings, and ready and willing to be comfortably assimilated into the particular landscape of which they inevitably form a part". Williams-Ellis asked for new-build which was "in a rough sort of harmony with its setting", which "would broadcast nothing alien to its environment or violently shocking to our senses .... Well-mannered new cottages, for instance, being added on to an old village would do their utmost to round off and complete the picture (probably a quiet and homely one) already composed by their predecessors. They would bear themselves discreetly and with great circumspection in the hope of proving welcome additions to the family."

Interestingly, Williams-Ellis was particularly exercised by the proliferation of railings, an extremely prominent feature in a large number of Spencer's postwar works. "We are a nation of railers-off and railers-in – the Englishman's home is his cage," he bemoaned: "They are even placed waist high on bridges and around flower beds where everything else invites the leisurely to lean and linger."[18] To Spencer, however, the cage was a haven of safety from the outside world, the railings creating a magical space in which God and his angels ... could manifest themselves to him in uninterrupted solitude. Spencer's apparent obsession with iron railings – which play a prominent part in pictures as diverse as *Zacharias and Elizabeth* (1913–14, Tate), *Christ carrying the Cross* (1920, Tate), *Sarah Tubb and the Heavenly Visitors* (fig. 37) and *The Dustman* or *The Lovers* (fig. 5) – was far more enthusiastic than Williams-Ellis's diatribe. In *Sarah Tubb* the white-clad visitors admit the legendary Cookham visionary into a small garden through an iron gate. *Gardens in the Pound* of 1936 (fig. 6) elevates the humble iron railing to centre stage in the composition, as a representation of the trammelling of nature – the geranium

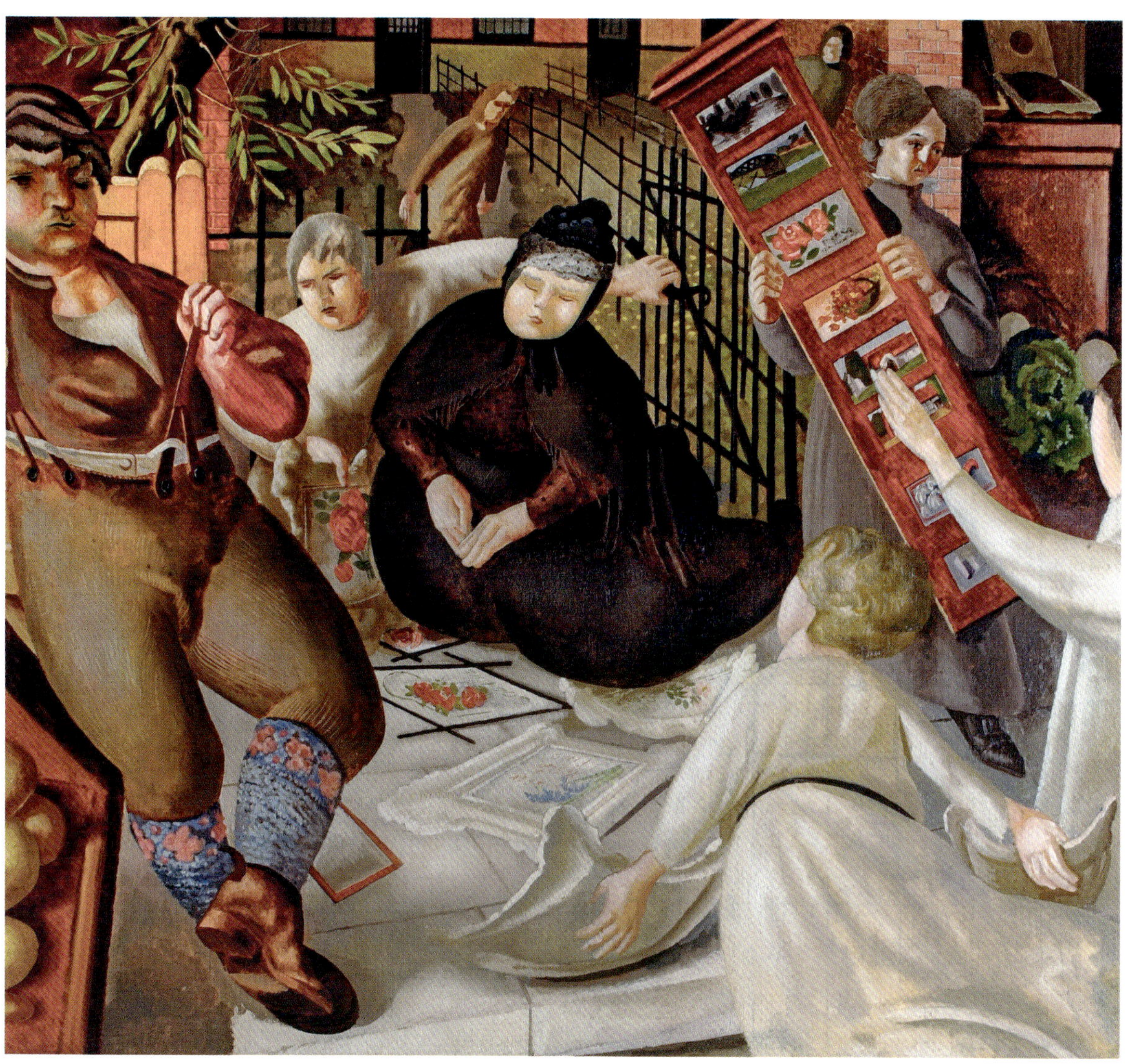

37
STANLEY SPENCER
Sarah Tubb and the Heavenly Visitors, 1933
Oil on canvas, 94 x 102.4 cm
Stanley Spencer Gallery, Cookham

beds are closely circumscribed, not just by the railings but also by gravel, brick and terracotta – and a synecdoche for the proud householders whose neat homes we can just make out. In *Cookham Rise: Cottages* of the same year (fig. 38), the same concept is used, less brutally, for the wooden fencing.

Spencer's painting *Cookham Rise* of 1938 (fig. 39) particularly demonstrates the links the artist was trying to make between the development of his immediate Chiltern landscape and the carnage of the First World War. Here the newly defined rear gardens of the well-built, brand-new council houses fight for precedence with the surrounding fields. The screen of trees in the foreground acts as a curtain. Indeed, Spencer exaggerates the height of his viewpoint to make his message that much clearer. (This elevated viewpoint, looking down past a lush, detailed foreground to a distant horizon was, as Keith Bell has noted, a favourite compositional device of the Pre-Raphaelite painters.)[19]

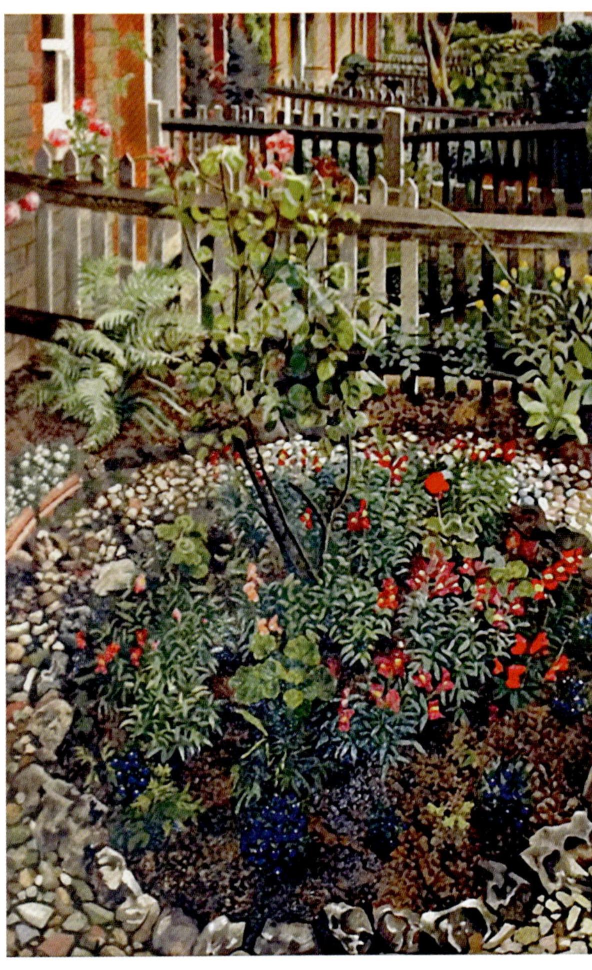

38
STANLEY SPENCER
Cookham Rise: Cottages, 1936
Oil on canvas, 75.6 x 49.5 cm
Lady Margaret Hall, Oxford

Spencer's view of the houses in Grange Road presumably originates from a point adjacent to the railway line; yet in reality the ground does not descend as sharply as his painting suggests. Pull the curtain aside, and behind it we see what is happening to the homely topography of rural England. The eye is instantly drawn to the new gardens' temporary marker posts, advancing like soldiers down the gentle slope. Already the gardens are beginning to produce the first fruits and vegetables. The occupation of the countryside proceeds apace.

Spencer's concerns were reflected by a near neighbour of his. Just a few months after Spencer finished *Cookham Rise*, George Orwell published his novel about the loss of place and local – and national – identity, *Coming Up for Air*. His anti-hero, George Bowling, revisits his childhood home of Binfield in Berkshire – just a few miles away from, and roughly the same size as, Spencer's Cookham – and finds that "The Mill Farm had vanished", and in its stead "was all houses, houses, little red cubes of houses all alike, with privet hedges and asphalt paths leading up to the front door".[20] Orwell's own boyhood had been spent near Cookham, in towns and villages on the Berkshire–Oxfordshire border. Indeed, Orwell was only twelve years younger than his near contemporary, Spencer. His

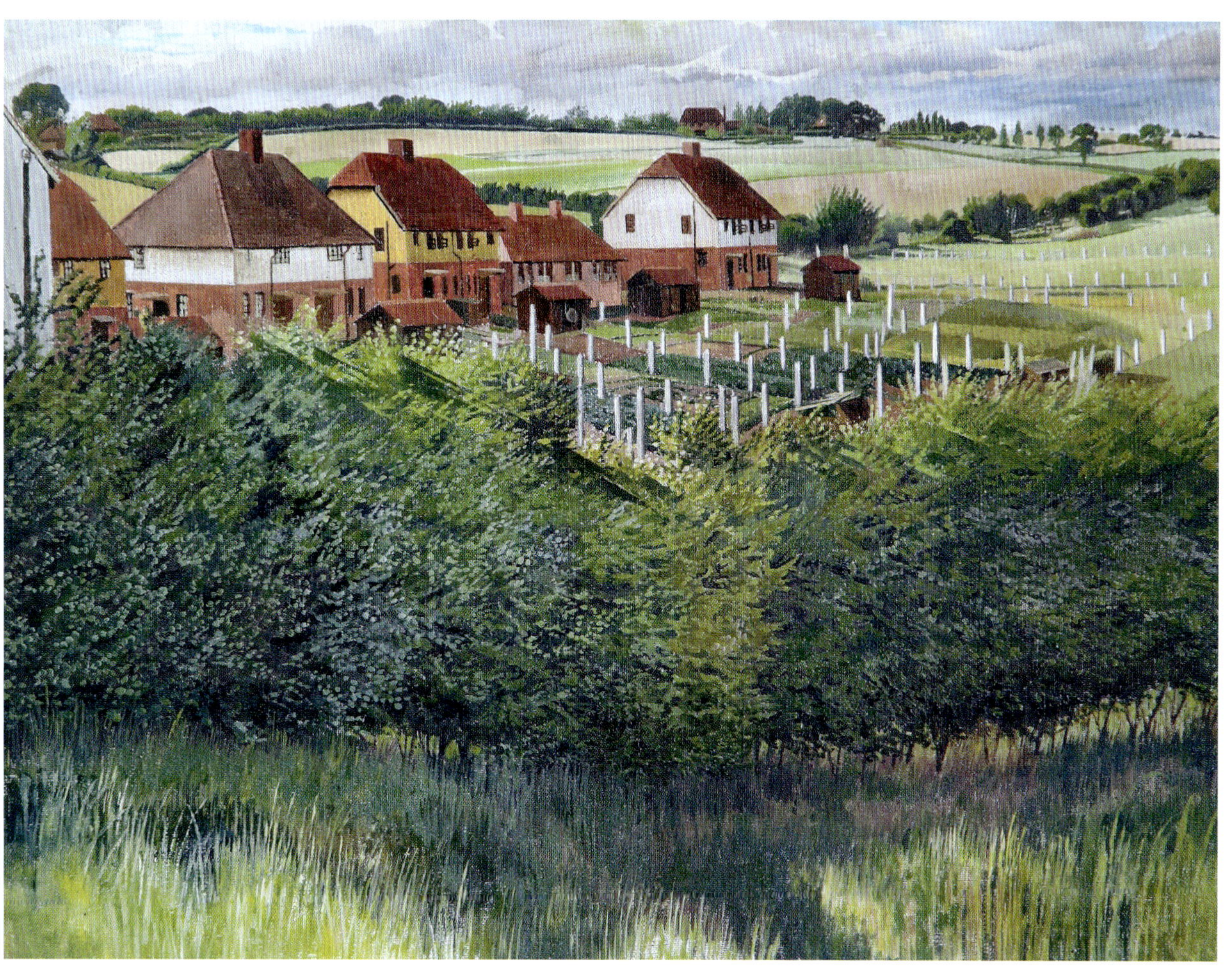

39
STANLEY SPENCER
Cookham Rise, 1938
Oil on canvas, 45.7 × 70 cm
Leamington Art Gallery

novel, like Spencer's Cookham views, is a "eulogy for the remembered village".[21]

Spencer's village scenes were perhaps deceptively gentle, but they never depicted overt conflict. Spencer was not one for bold, melodramatic statements; even his view of the First World War was "one in which the violence is understated".[22] In *Cookham Rise* he cheerfully celebrates the red clay tiles, the well-laid brickwork and the freshly painted render of the new, council-built homes – constructed in an idiom which was comfortably settled within the English building tradition, and one which found its inspiration in the Georgian and Victorian homes of the old village centre – while simultaneously recording the increasing tension between architecture, garden and landscape. The council homes blend easily with their natural context, most of their building materials having been locally sourced. They are of the same vernacular building tradition as the older house glimpsed on the horizon.

Even before Spencer's death in 1959, however, the tension he illustrates in *Cookham Rise* was beginning to escalate. Cookham Rise itself, an outlying, western extension of the historic village which had grown up around the Great Western Railway station, had by the 1950s begun to be intensively developed, and the

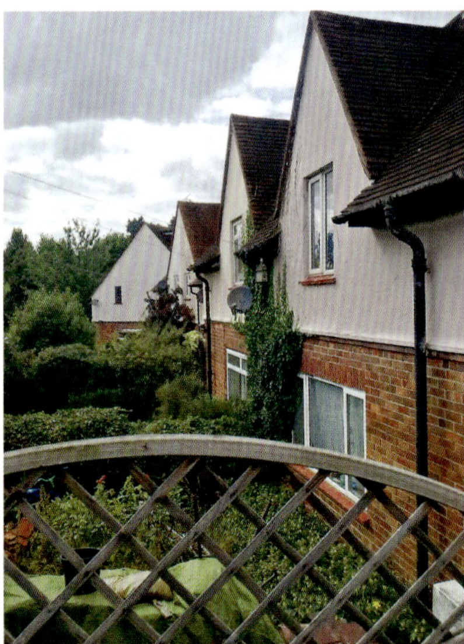

40–41
Cookham Rise today

fields and footpaths that Spencer portrayed obliterated. By 1959, poor-quality council housing had begun to be erected to the east of Grange Road, obscuring the view of the fine new council houses on Grange Road that Spencer had celebrated in *Cookham Rise*, and designed to far less exacting standards. And not long after Spencer's death, a hideous parade of shops was built to the east of the station, designed in a perfunctory manner that completely ignored local building traditions and materials, and which looked for its inspiration more to the New Towns of Stevenage and Harlow than to the Thames Valley. During the 1980s, partly as a result of Margaret Thatcher's policy of promoting council house sales, the *Cookham Rise* homes were themselves extended and 'improved'. Today they stand adorned with uPVC double glazing and large extensions, submerged within the characterless and mean developments of the postwar years, and constituting a silent but powerful testimony to the despoliation of the gentle England so beloved by Spencer and Orwell (figs. 40–41).

The wartime allegory of *Cookham Rise* is, in the context of his recent experience, entirely understandable. When serving overseas on the Salonica Front in 1917, Spencer was sustained by his visions of Cookham – its postage-stamp gardens, its modest but sturdy homes, and its fine brick walls. "The shop is over shadowed," he recalled beatifically of his home environment, "by a clump of pollarded elms which stands just outside the old red bricked wall which is built round Mr Waller's house. Appearing above the elms and part way between them & a Ceda [*sic*] tree which rises from the garden enclosure formed by the wall are Mr Waller's malt house and their slate roofs."[23]

The First World War affected Spencer deeply – not only his own war service in Macedonia, but also the death of his brother, Sydney, on the Western Front in October 1918, only a month before the Armistice. After the war Stanley acknowledged that even his Christian faith was shaken: he had, he admitted to John Rothenstein, now "got the wind up about Hell".[24] Yet, when Spencer returned to the village in 1932, he was reassured to find it little changed from his

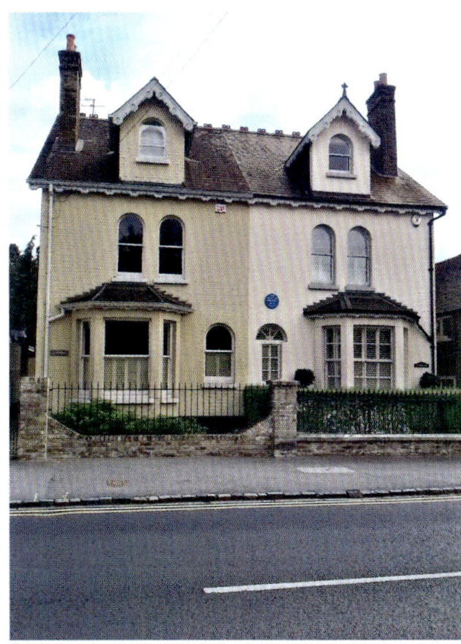

42
Fernlea and Belmont, Cookham

boyhood and wartime recollections. As his brother Gilbert later observed, "change came slowly to Cookham .... Even the railway had brought few changes."[25]

Cookham's comforting architectural idiom, a restful, gentle language of brick and tile, dominated almost all of Spencer's paintings – even those which dealt with more overtly religious subjects. In the second version of his work *The Betrayal* (fig. 36), the architecture of Cookham is just as important to the composition as the central figures of Saint Peter and the High Priest's servant. The cramped back gardens behind Cookham's schoolroom are tightly defined by brick and rendered walls, by slate and ceramic tiles, and by angular, knapped-flint panels. Indeed, the abrupt physicality of the flint panels is used to underline the violence of Saint Peter's unexpected outburst, to which they offer a deliberately fractured background. Stanley and his brother Gilbert, accompanied by an unidentified girl, cling for comfort to the architecture of these sheltered spaces as they watch the disturbing scene, which takes place barely yards away. They shrink against the wall of the corrugated-iron shed – or, in the case of the girl, peep over the gauged brick coping of the absurdly high wall – while the retreating apostles themselves scurry between two equally lofty brick walls for protection, one or two summoning up enough courage to offer anxious looks backwards. (Christ's apostles by no means offer a heroic example in this picture.) Architecture lends both reassurance and a refuge, even as its familiar, placid forms play host to events which are both passionate and surreal.

Spencer's architectural vision was a markedly traditional one. Late in his life he recalled seeing builders at work in Hampstead, and criticized them for using a wooden frame to construct a brick arch: "Personally I think they are horrible mechanical devices", he said of the former, "and are responsible for arches now being so symmetrical, when the old builders used to use their eye."[26]

Stanley Spencer's background was rooted in building. His grandfather, Julius, had set up as a master builder in Cookham around 1830, and about twenty years later built a pair of stout, brick semi-detached homes near the village centre for his sons William (called Fernlea or, later, Fernley) and Julius junior (Belmont) upon the occasion of their two marriages (fig. 42). William, Stanley's father, continued in the same profession. As a result, Stanley and his brothers often played in the family builder's yard as children: "There was sand still lying around, with which we used to play", he later reminisced, remembering how "Tiles were stacked against the sides of a tottering building".[27]

Having been steeped in the builder's trade since infancy, Spencer was fascinated by the properties and colours of Cookham's principal building materials – brick, terracotta and iron. As Keith Bell has noted, he painted even the most humble architectural features "with the same sensuous enjoyment of colour and texture that is lavished on flowering shrubs [and] trees".[28]

The compositions of his Cookham garden pictures often hinge on the contrast between the ruddy reds of the locally sourced Buckinghamshire bricks and tiles and the vibrant greens of nature. He particularly revelled in the contrasting hues of fired bricks, and featured them prominently in a number of his works. It is somewhat ironic, then, that at some point after Spencer's death the brick fronts of the two Spencer semis, Fernlea and Belmont, were crudely and unwisely covered in paint – a visually unfortunate and structurally unsound finish which Stanley, and his father and grandfather, would surely have abhorred. The materials and buildings the artist portrayed were also innately English; indeed, for Spencer, their forms epitomized the understated English values he held so dearly. Writing to Edward Marsh, who had bought the 1914 landscape *Cookham* (Tullie House and Art Gallery, Carlisle), he stated: "I know I was reading English Ballads at the time and feeling a new and personal value of the Englishness of England."[29]

To Spencer, the border between his very English concept of nature and the interventions of vernacular architecture was a particularly fascinating one. Indeed, the importance of boundaries in his pictures provides us with an interesting glimpse not only into Stanley's childhood, which he seems to have spent largely in the builder's yard (looking back to the turn of the century, he recalled that "fun and games with cast iron was by then very much in vogue, and my grandfather made generous use of this material"),[30] but also into his apparent obsession with compartmentalizing and safeguarding his environment. The peculiar attraction of Cookham's gardens to him lay partly in the fact that they were small, and could be easily defended from unwanted visitors by high brick walls, stout wooden fences and formidable iron gates, the dimensions of which are often deliberately exaggerated in his pictures.

Walls played a leading part in Spencer's oeuvre. They were rarely meant to serve as mere background, but represented crucial elements in the picture's story – defining the garden space, ensuring privacy, and preventing others from seeing or overhearing. In *The Betrayal* (fig. 36), the brick walls which delineate and compartmentalize the back gardens of Cookham are, as already noted, crucial to the action in the picture. In *Boatbuilder's Yard, Cookham* of 1936 (fig. 15), the crumbling brick wall dominates the composition, cutting the picture in two and surreally dividing the garden patio, with its symbolic fishtank and mystical fish, from the picturesquely chaotic boatyard beyond.

Even in Spencer's later works of the 1940s and 1950s, walls, gates and fences played a prominent role, but the tension between nature and architecture seems

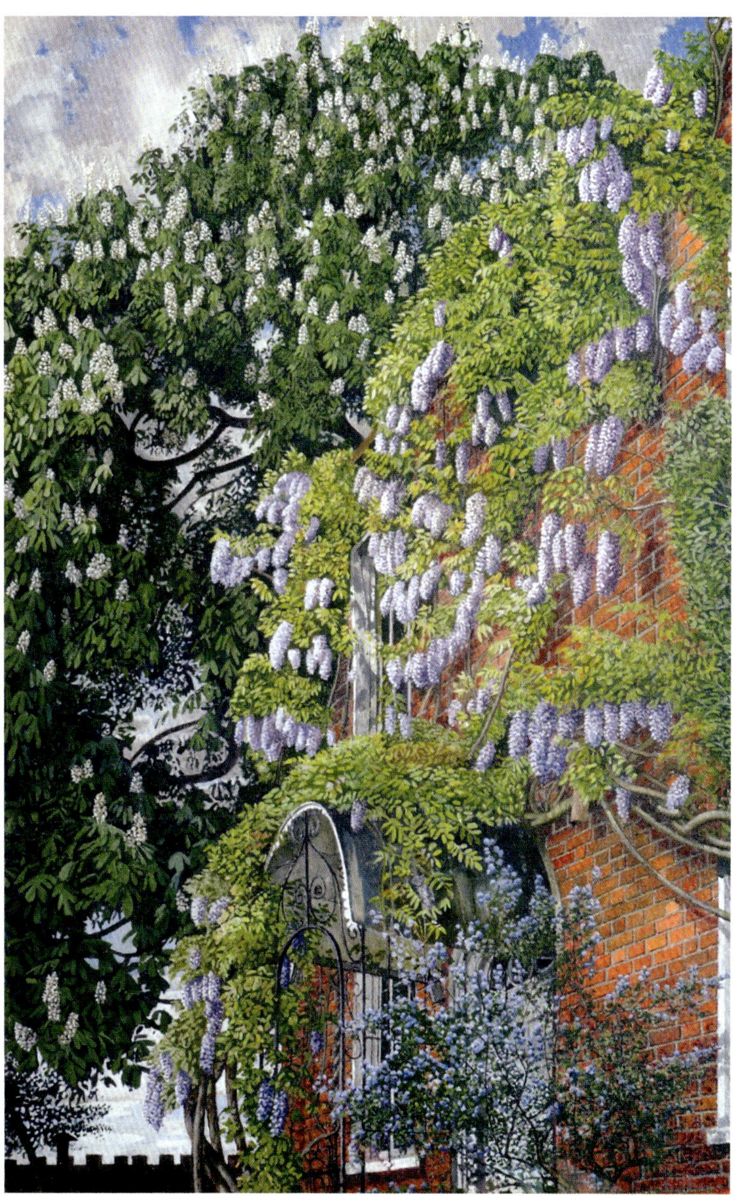

43
STANLEY SPENCER
Wisteria at Englefield, 1954
Oil on canvas, 76 x 51 cm
Private collection

to have softened, and become less adversarial. For example, in three works of the mid 1950s – *Wallflowers* (1954, private collection), *Wisteria at Englefield* (fig. 43) and *Rock Roses, Old Lodge, Taplow* (1957, private collection) – nature triumphs over the brickwork courses, but in a rather more sentimental and mawkish manner than the artist had demonstrated in his interwar views.

The garden that these walls encompassed had itself always provided a refuge for young Stanley. At the bottom of the family's own Cookham garden, his sister, Annie, had run a pretend school:

> It was a lovely spot really, there was the school and ... in our garden a fairish number of trees. There was a lovely yew tree, the kind of yew tree that branches

> out from the base and goes out in, making a most lovely shape ... and behind you could see the walnut tree going up, soaring away for ever like a huge great sort of planet Jupiter.[31]

Most importantly, to the adult Spencer, every Cookham garden was a vision of heaven, glimpsed from outside:

> as a child I used to peep through chinks & cracks in fences, etc & catch glimpses of these gardens of Eden of which there was a profusion at Cookham. From these glimpses I used to get, I assumed that some sort of saint or very wonderful person lived there.[32]

The more he understood and was able to communicate these visions, Spencer believed, the nearer he came to personal salvation. "The early days of art experience," he wrote in 1948, "had shown that the nearer one could approach to nature itself, the nearer one came to these personal desires & wishes & the fulfilment of them."[33] He sought to find his personal heaven in the back gardens and front areas of his own village. As Keith Bell has observed, "Stanley Spencer did not start out by wanting to become an artist, but by wanting to communicate something about his native village, Cookham".[34]

Spencer identified himself very closely with the streets and gardens of his home village. As early as 1908 his colleagues gave him the nickname 'Cookham', a moniker which stuck with him for the rest of his life.[35] By the 1930s he had come to see the whole of Cookham as a village in heaven, and its private gardens as manifestations of the meaning of nature. Even the humblest garden could provide him with heavenly inspiration: "Places in Cookham mean specific spots ... in which he finds, or suddenly found, an ecstasy of sensation" – such as the "many apertures" in his own garden's fir tree which "seem holy and secret" and which "greatly excites my imagination".[36]

As a result, Spencer's garden and landscape views were not of dramatic mountains or lakes. His wartime service in Macedonia, for example, did not prompt him to embark on a series of grand European landscapes. Nor did he tour England in search of a more challenging topography. He preferred instead the local and the familiar, the russets and greens of his home village. On his return to England he acknowledged "the liking I have for my usual & more familiar abodes, namely my being able to make some sort of home or nest in it". Such familiar views and visions were extremely important to Spencer. In 1941 he admitted that, when he travelled further afield (which he did more rarely now), "having photos of these [Cookham] landscapes is most important to me". The gardens, walls and railings of Cookham continued to accompany, safeguard and inspire him for the rest of his life.

NOTES

STANLEY SPENCER'S GARDENS

Keith Bell, pp. 18–37

I would like to thank to the staff of the Stanley Spencer Gallery, Cookham – in particular Ann Danks; Adrian Glew and the staff of the Tate Gallery Archives; and Candace Savage, the editor of my essay.

1 Artist's notes written in 1942 for an exhibition at the Leicester Galleries, London.
2 Letter to Dudley Tooth, dated April 1940 and written at the White Hart Inn, Leonard Stanley, Gloucestershire. The painting in question was probably Cottage Garden, Leonard Stanley (see Bell 1992, p. 288; private collection).
3 See the chapter on landscape in Bell 1992, and Bartram 1999.
4 Tate Archives (hereafter TA), 733.2.1.
5 TA 733.3.21.
6 TA 733.3.45.
7 TA 733.3.1.
8 TA 733.3.1.
9 Bell 1992, p. 250.
10 TA 733.10.143.
11 Bell 1992, p. 272.
12 Tate Archives, Spencer-Tooth correspondence.
13 Bell 1992, p. 279
14 *Ibid.*
15 TA 733.3. 39, 231.
16 TA 733.3.7.
17 Interview, *A Village Remembers Stanley Spencer*, CD produced by Chrissy Rosenthal and Ann Danks, Stanley Spencer Gallery.
18 TA 733.3.1,1.

"HAPPY ENGLAND"

Martin Postle, pp. 38–53

1 Nicholas Alfrey, 'On Garden Colour', in London, Belfast and Manchester 2004, p. 37.
2 Helmreich 2002, p. 77.
3 *The Times* obituary of Helen Allingham, 26 September 1926.
4 Helmreich 2002, p. 47.
5 London, Belfast and Manchester 2004, no. 76, p. 162.
6 Elliott 1986, pp. 205–09.
7 Bell 1992, p. 284.
8 London, Belfast and Manchester 2004, p. 13.
9 Burchardt 2002, p. 236.
10 See Bartram 1999; also Stephen Daniels in London, Belfast and Manchester 2004, p. 87.
11 Crouch and Ward 1988, p. 197; see also the Departmental Committee of Enquiry into Allotments, 1969 (the 'Thorpe Report').
12 Rothenstein 1984, vol. 2, p. 167.
13 Ben Tufnell in London, Belfast and Manchester 2004, p. 226; see also Joan Warburton, 'A Painter's Progress: Part of a Life 1920–87', unpublished MS, Tate Archive.
14 Beth Chatto, 'Sir Cedric Morris, Artist-Gardener', *Hortus*, no. 1, 1987, p. 15.
15 See Elizabeth Bulkeley, 'Charles Mahoney 1903–1968', in London 1999, pp. 9–10.
16 For the Brockley School murals, which are still *in situ*, see Powers 1987; Clarke 2006, pp. 28–43.
17 See Clarke 2006, *passim*.
18 For the Mahoney-Dunbar correspondence see Clarke 2006, pp. 44ff. and 80, note 6.
19 Evelyn Dunbar to Charles Mahoney, September 1935, MS private collection. See London, Belfast and Manchester 2004, p. 18, fig. 7.
20 John Rothenstein, *Studio*, 1936, p. 149. See also London, Belfast and Manchester 2004, p. 76.
21 London 1999, p. 61.
22 Oxford 1975, p. 12.
23 Lousley 1946, p. 413; see also London, Belfast and Manchester 2004, p. 116.
24 Ben Tufnell in London, Belfast and Manchester 2004, p. 229.
25 Khoroche 2007, p. 91.

LANDSCAPES AND GARDENS OF THE LONG WEEKEND

Jeremy Gould, pp. 54–75

1 See Graves and Hodge 1941, which chronicled the major events of the period from contemporary memoirs and newspapers.
2 The figures vary. These and the following statistics come from Oliver, Davis and Bentley 1981, p. 13, and Ian Davis, 'One of the Greatest Evils ... Dunroamin and the Modern Movement', in *ibid.*, p. 46.
3 Young 1943, p. 22. Young commented that England and Wales had 703 people per square mile, ahead of Belgium at 702 people per square mile, Holland at 633, France at 197 and USA at 43. The figure for England alone was 766.
4 This figure comes from the Scott Report on the countryside of 1942 and is quoted in Young 1943, p. 35. It is a gross figure excluding land returned to agriculture from other uses which Young estimates at about 10 per cent "immediately before 1939". Ian Davis in Oliver, Davis and Bentley 1981, p. 48, has the figure at 70,000 acres.
5 The Conservative MP for Chelmsford, Ernest Pretyman, in 1919, quoted in Swenarton 1981, p. 86. For an account of the Tudor Walters report see 'A New Standard for State Housing', in Swenarton 1981, pp. 88–111.
6 F.J. Osborn in the Preface to Ebenezer Howard's *Garden Cities of To-Morrow* (Howard 1946, p. 26). *Garden Cities of To-Morrow* was first published in 1902, slightly revising the original *To-Morrow: A Peaceful Path to Reform* of 1898.
7 George Cadbury quoted by Swenarton 1981, p. 8, and taken from Cornes 1905, p. 71. Housing plot sizes at Bournville were 1/8th acre (605 square yards) and at New Earswick gardens were 350 square yards.
8 *Municipal Journal*, vol. 15, 1 June 1906, p. 595, quoted by Swenarton 1981, p. 14.
9 For an account of these London estates see Roger Bowdler, 'Between the Wars: 1914–1940', in Saint 1999, pp. 102–29. The 'cottage' estates and other contemporary housing by the LCC are illustrated in Cox 1931.
10 See Ravetz 1995, pp. 176–89.
11 Young 1934, p. 373, quoted in Ravetz 1995, p. 181.
12 Phrase taken from the definition of the Garden City of the Garden Cities and Town Planning Association and quoted in de Soissons 1988, p. 37.
13 Quoted from an advertisement for Welwyn Garden City in *Punch*, summer 1920, and reproduced in de Soissons 1988, p. 39.
14 This idea came from America. It had been suggested and rejected by the Tudor Walters committee since "in this country ... there appears to exist a general desire for some enclosure". Tudor Walters Report quoted in

Ian Bentley, 'Individualism or Community?', in Oliver, Davis and Bentley 1981, p. 112.

15 The information for this paragraph comes from personal observation, Soissons 1988, pp. 37–91, and Osborn and Whittick 1963, pp. 33–52. Frederick Osborn was secretary and estates manager of Welwyn Garden City Ltd from 1920 to 1936.

16 This is discussed in Ravetz 1995, pp. 176–80.

17 Lindsay and Washington 1952, p. 255. Mr Middleton's programme was *In Your Garden*.

18 S. Martin Gaskell, 'Gardens for the Working Class: Victorian Practical Pleasure', *Victorian Studies*, vol. 23, no. 4, summer 1980, p. 483, quoted by Ravetz 1995, p. 177.

19 See Ian Bentley, 'The Owner Makes his Mark', pp. 136–53, and Paul Oliver, 'The Galleon on the Front Door', pp. 154–72, in Oliver, Davis and Bentley 1981.

20 The sunburst is a recurring motif in the architecture of the 1920s, symbolizing birth or renewal. See Rice and Evans 1972.

21 Only the more expensive houses in the 1930s would have included an integral single garage designed for the width of an Austin 10 or a Morris 8. Otherwise a space would be left between adjacent semis for the owner to add a prefabricated wooden or asbestos panel garage. In meaner layouts, only a common, shared driveway would be left between adjacent houses, and the paired garages would be relegated to the back garden.

22 C. Geoffrey Holme, 'Designing the New Garden', in Mercer 1937, p. 9.

23 The Metal Agencies Co Ltd (MAC) was the largest builders' merchant in Bristol.

24 James Veitch & Sons had nurseries at Feltham, Chelsea and Coombe Hill before the war and at Exeter and Alphington in Devon in the 1920s. By the beginning of the century, they had become specialists in orchids, ferns, conifers and roses. Sir Harry Veitch was one of the founders of the Royal Horticultural Society's Chelsea Flower Show in 1913.

25 See Paul Oliver in Oliver, Davis and Bentley 1981, pp. 168–72.

26 Lancaster 1938, pp. 60, 62 and 68.

27 'By-pass Variegated', in Lancaster 1938, p. 68.

28 Quest-Ritson 2001, p. 229.

29 Cherry and Rogers 1996, p. 49.

30 Young 1943, p. 29. Young notes that the number of male workers fell from 587,000 to 472,000 – a drop of nearly 20 per cent.

31 *Ibid*., p. 30. By June 1939 the average agricultural wage had risen to £1.60–£1.87 and the industrial wage to £2.15–£3.00.

32 According to Paul Oliver in Oliver, Davis and Bentley 1981, p. 14. Graves and Hodge 1941, p. 173, have this as £5.00–£10.00 a week, indicating that the 1930s especially was a time of inflation that was not reflected in rural wage levels.

33 Graves and Hodge 1941, pp. 185–90.

34 This list from Abercrombie 1943, pp. 228–29, first published in 1933. Support came from the many new organizations which reflected a changing society: the Youth Hostels Association (founded 1930), the Ramblers' Association (1935), the Camping Club of Great Britain and Ireland (re-formed in 1919 and with a Caravan Section in 1933) and the National Trust (founded in 1895 but in the 1930s with a membership approaching 7,000 and, from the late 1930s, taking over country estates and historic landscapes).

35 Information from the CPRE website www.cpre.org.uk/about/achievements1920.

36 Williams-Ellis 1928/1996, p. 16.

37 *Ibid*., pp. 148–49.

38 *Ibid*., p. 148. Williams-Ellis cites the village of Clandon in Surrey as being exemplary and, characteristically, attacks the Welsh for being idle since "in Wales a garden means a patch of potatoes and black-currant bushes, flowers being regarded as an amiable eccentricity, though perhaps a little worldly".

39 In this he is referring to another influential polemic of the time – A. Trystan Edwards's *Good & Bad Manners in Architecture*, 1924.

40 William Walter Wood, 'Glorious Devon', *The Architectural Review*, September 1929, p. 111. Wood was head of the Department of Architecture at Plymouth School of Arts and Crafts.

41 See Prof. Patrick Abercrombie MA, 'National Parks: A Resumé of the Position', in *Report of the British Association of Science 98th meeting*, Bristol 1930.

42 Young 1943, pp. 49–50. Young notes that all agricultural buildings were excluded from the 1932 act and that the 1935 act was further complicated by the approvals required by "another Government Department" (the Ministry of Transport) in the process.

43 The London green belt is discussed in Jackson 1973, pp. 315–18. The legislation of the period is discussed by Cherry and Rogers 1996, 'Regulation and Planning', pp. 65–69.

44 Abercrombie 1943, p. 21. *Feng shui* is one of the entries in Williams-Ellis's 'Devil's Dictionary', which quotes Abercrombie's *The Preservation of Rural England* at length.

45 *Ibid*., pp. 123–27. See Abercrombie, Humble and Johnson 1922.

46 Sharp 1936, p. 86.

47 Sharp 1940, p. 122.

48 Sharp 1936, p. 100.

49 This process is nicely parodied in Lancaster 1936, showing how the mythical Pelvis Bay had changed by the 1930s. The joke was repeated for the town of Drayneflete in *Drayneflete Revealed*, published in 1949.

50 Rasmussen's *London: The Unique City* (1934) extolled the virtues of the plain brick terraced houses, the squares and parks of the eighteenth-century city. John Summerson was lecturing on London in the 1930s but his *Georgian London* did not appear until 1945.

51 Henry Ernest Milner was the son of the firm's founder, Edward Milner, who had been apprenticed to Paxton at Chatsworth. His father, Henry Milner, was a gardener and porter at Chatsworth.

52 Peter Youngman records that Abercrombie "never took an active part in the affairs of the Institute". See Youngman 1985, p. 51.

53 Title taken from Brown 1982.

54 Robinson's with photo-engravings but Jekyll's with half-tone photographs and in *Gardens for Small Country Houses* clear architectural drawings of plans and details.

55 A wonderful collection of these is illustrated in Elliott 1995.

56 Seen clearly in Mawson's Wood in South Tawton, Devon (1898–1907): tennis lawn, bowling green, croquet lawn, kitchen garden, orchard, lily pond and sundial court are all axially arranged and rectilinear with the house, each framed with hedges and some with pergola walks. See Mawson 1994. A full biography of Mawson is provided in Waymark 2009.

57 Admission fees for the National Gardens Scheme funded the Queen's Institute of District Nursing from 1928. The 'Yellow Book', listing and illustrating the gardens, was published from 1932. From the outset over 600 gardens were listed.

58 These gardens, designers and owners are well described in Brown 1999.

59 See Quest-Ritson 2001, pp. 229–33. They did survive, of course, but were taken over by charitable trusts or the National Trust after the Second World War.

60 Russell Page, 'Gardens that Look Inevitable', from an unknown American journal of 1980 accessed on www.scribd.com.

61 *My Garden, Illustrated* was a monthly periodical owned by a farmer, Bernard Martin. Cane contributed articles from 1915, became editor in 1918 and owner/editor in 1919. Information from Webber 1975. Cane was only briefly a member of the ILA.

62 Taken from an advertisement in 1937 for George Dillistone FILA, landscape architect, in Mercer 1937.

63 Youngman 1987, p. 107.

64 Correspondence between Dillistone and Sir Pendrill Varrier-Jones of Papworth Hall, Cambridgeshire for the design of a garden in Herefordshire, 29 May, 5 June and 8 June 1934, Cambridgeshire Archive Services, ref: 1383/8/6.

65 Dillistone 1929. For the Iris Society, he edited *Dykes on Irises: A Reprint of the Contributions of the Late W.R. Dykes, L-es-L., to Various Journals and Periodicals during the Last Twenty Years of his Life* (see Dillistone 1930). He designed Goddards garden in York for

Noel Goddard Terry of the York chocolate family in 1927.

66 The book and Jellicoe's career are discussed in Harvey 1998.

67 Including articles on historic European gardens, Pompeii, the theatre at Herrenhausen, Italian villas, Le Nôtre's Sceaux, French and Portuguese gardens, and on contemporary gardens such as Gravetye and Hidcote. See Jacques 1985, pp. 27–43.

68 See Jacques 1985, pp. 29–31. Christopher Hussey had published *The Picturesque* in 1927. Dorothy Stroud lectured on Brown in the 1930s but her book *Capability Brown* was not published until 1950.

69 Le Corbusier 1946, p. 9. This was originally published by John Rodker in 1927, as translated by the English architect, Frederick Etchells. *Towards a New Architecture* was Etchells's (mis)translation of Le Corbusier's *Vers une Architecture*, originally published in 1923.

70 Paul Nash, 'Going Modern and Being British', *The Weekend Review*, 12 March 1932, pp. 322–23, quoted by Sam Smiles, 'Refuge and Regeneration: Devon's Twentieth-Century Identity', in Smiles 1998.

71 See Gould 1996. The Gazetteer records about 700 houses and sites and includes some later houses that had shallow-pitched roofs.

72 For these see Imbert 1993.

73 'Daily Mail Ideal Home Exhibition' supplement to the *Daily Mail*, 16 February 1928, illustrated in Ryan 1997, p. 58. Ryan records that the house was designed by S. Rowland Pierce and R.A. Duncan, but Duncan's firm at the time was Percy Tubbs, Son & Duncan, as recorded in the *Daily Mail*. Jellicoe's garden was designed with J.C. Shepherd (information from Alan Powers).

74 This is illustrated in Imbert 1993, p. 97. The house was designed by Jean-Charles Moreux and Paul Vera, and was exhibited at the Salon d'Automne, Paris, in 1924.

75 The house was published in *The Architectural Review*, Raymond McGrath's *Twentieth-Century Houses* (1934) and F.R.S. Yorke's *The Modern House* (1934). McGrath and Yorke published other contemporary German houses of a similar type and setting. It is described in Heinze-Greenberg 1999.

76 Examples include Samuel & Harding's By-the-Links, Bromley (1934–35), Christopher Nicholson's Kit's Close, Fawley (1936–37), Oliver Hill's Landfall, Poole (1936–37), and Maxwell Fry's Miramonte, Kingston (1936–37).

77 Published in English for the first time; see Le Corbusier, 'The Town and the House', *The Architectural Review*, vol. 64, 1928, pp. 223ff. Mendelsohn's houses, of course, were firmly rooted to the ground.

78 Most of the houses mentioned here are illustrated in Powers 2005. The gardens are included in Jane Brown, 'Britain in the 1930s', in Brown 2000, pp. 48–71.

79 Information in Jacques and Woudstra 2009.

80 Bentley Wood is discussed in Jacques and Woudstra 2009, and in Powers 2001.

81 John Summerson in introduction to Dannatt 1959, p. 17.

82 See *The Architectural Review*, January 1939, p. 42; February 1939, pp. 95–96; March 1939, p. 147; April 1939, pp. 39, 173 – all beautifully drawn in black and white by Gordon Cullen. The 'Architects' Plants' were subsequently incorporated into later editions of *Gardens in the Modern Landscape*.

83 Jack Pritchard, the entrepreneur for the project, in Pritchard 1984, p. 105.

84 W.A. Eden, 'The English Tradition in the Countryside III: The Re-birth of the Tradition', *The Architectural Review*, May 1935, p. 194.

85 Le Corbusier's *The City of To-morrow* (*Urbanisme*) was published in English by John Rodker in 1929.

86 Christopher Tunnard, 'The Case for the Common Garden', *The Architectural Review*, September 1938, pp. 109–16. A shortened version of the article was included in *Gardens in the Modern Landscape*.

87 The gardens at Römerstadt were designed by Leberecht Migge, who is not named and had remained almost unknown until David H. Haney's comprehensive biography, *When Modern was Green: Life and Work of Landscape Architect Leberecht Migge*, Routledge, Abingdon, 2010. The Neubühl Estate (1930–32) was designed by members of the Swiss Werkbund.

88 Maxwell Fry paraphrased in *Landscape & Garden*, spring 1939, and quoted in Gordon Patterson, 'Planting and Garden Design', in Harvey and Rettig 1985, p. 94.

89 John Gloag, 'The Suburban Scene', in Williams-Ellis 1938, p. 199.

90 Richards 1946/1973, p. 13.

91 Abercrombie was a member of the Barlow Commission on the Distribution of the Urban Population (1941), where he called for the establishment of a central planning authority. The Uthwatt Report on Compensation and Betterment (1941) set out the parameters for the compulsory purchase and valuation of war-damaged development land after the Second World War. Essentially it allowed local authorities to purchase large areas of inner-city land and initiate comprehensive redevelopment on a scale that was impossible before the war.

92 Lewis Mumford, 'The Social Basis of the New Urban Order', in Mumford 1938, p. 428.

STANLEY SPENCER'S ARCHITECTURE

Steven Parissien, pp. 76–90

1 I am indebted to Professor Keith Bell, Dr Martin Postle and Professor Duncan Robinson for their advice and encouragement both of this essay and of the associated exhibition held at Compton Verney in 2011 – the original idea for which emanated from Dr Postle.

2 Bell 1992, p. 239.

3 *Ibid*., p. 272.

4 *Ibid*., p. 278.

5 *Ibid*.

6 "Having finished his quota of landscapes, he moved on to Hampstead ..." (Collis 1972, p. 103.)

7 Stanley Spencer Papers, 733.2.87, quoted in Glew 2001, p. 202.

8 Rothenstein 1980, p. 70.

9 Quoted in McCarthy 1997, p. 28.

10 Stanley Spencer Papers, 8726.4.74, quoted in Glew 2001, p. 203.

11 Bell 1992, p. 284.

12 Harris 2010, p. 171.

13 *Ibid*.

14 *Times Literary Supplement*, 30 April 1938, p. 291, quoted in Harris 2010, pp. 172, 303.

15 Bryant 1990, p. 69.

16 Draper and Eden 1970, p. 52.

17 Stanley Spencer Papers, 882.1.

18 Williams-Ellis 1928, pp. 18, 20, 121, 133, 134, 168, 169.

19 Bell 1992, p. 240.

20 Orwell 1990, p. 73.

21 Harris 2010, p. 175.

22 McCarthy 1997, p. 30.

23 Rothenstein 1979, p. 17.

24 Rothenstein 1980, p. 56.

25 Spencer 1961, p. 27.

26 Tate Archive, Stanley Spencer Papers, 733.3.1, 96.

27 Spencer 1961, p. 13.

28 Bell 1992, p. 300.

29 Pople 1991, p. 70. Rothenstein 1979.

30 Spencer 1961, p. 13.

31 Stanley Spencer, 'Pictures of Childhood': BCC Radio talk given on 9 January 1955, quoted in Glew 2001, p. 22.

32 Stanley Spencer Papers, 733.2.87, quoted in Glew 2001, p. 203.

33 Stanley Spencer Papers, 733.2.67, quoted in Glew 2001, p. 229.

34 Bell 1980, p. 19.

35 Collis 1962, p. 17.

36 Pople 1991, p. 24; Rothenstein 1979, p. 18.

BIBLIOGRAPHY

ABERCROMBIE 1943
Patrick Abercrombie, *Town and Country Planning*, Oxford University Press, London, 1943

ABERCROMBIE, HUMBLE AND JOHNSON 1943
Patrick Abercrombie, Joseph Humble and Thomas H. Johnson, *The Doncaster Regional Planning Scheme*, Liverpool University Press and Hodder & Stoughton, London, 1922

BERTRAM 1999
Rob Bartram, 'The Enclosure of Nature in Stanley Spencer's *Hoe Garden Nursery*', *Ecumene*, vol. 6, no. 3, July 1999, pp. 341–59

BELL 1980
Keith Bell, *Stanley Spencer RA*, Royal Academy, London, 1980

BELL 1992
Keith Bell, *Stanley Spencer: A Complete Catalogue of the Paintings*, Phaidon Press, London, 1992

BROWN 1982
Jane Brown, *Gardens of a Golden Afternoon. The Story of a Partnership: Edwin Lutyens and Gertrude Jekyll*, Penguin, Harmondsworth, 1982

BROWN 1999
Jane Brown, *The English Garden through the Twentieth Century*, Garden Art Press, Woodbridge, 1999

BROWN 2000
Jane Brown, *The Modern Garden*, Thames & Hudson, London, 2000

BRYANT 1990
Julius Bryant, *The Iveagh Bequest, Kenwood*, The London Historic House Museums Trust, London, 1990

BURCHARDT 2002
Jeremy Burchardt, *The Allotment Movement in England, 1793–1873*, Boydell & Brewer, Woodbridge, 2002

CHERRY AND ROGERS 1996
Gordon E. Cherry and Alan Rogers, *Rural Change and Planning: England and Wales in the Twentieth Century*, E. & F.N. Spon, London, 1996

CLARK 2006
Gill Clarke, *Evelyn Dunbar: War and Country*, Sansom, Bristol, 2006

COLLIS 1962
Maurice Collis, *Stanley Spencer*, Harvill Press, London, 1962

COLLIS 1972
Louise Collis, *A Private View of Stanley Spencer*, Heinemann, London, 1972

CORNES 1905
J. Cornes, *Modern Housing in Town and Country*, Batsford, London, 1905

COX 1931
Montague H. Cox, *Housing 1928–30*, London County Council, 1931

CROUCH AND WARD 1988
David Crouch and Colin Ward, *The Allotment: Its Landscape and Culture*, Faber and Faber, London, 1988

DANNATT 1959
Trevor Dannatt, *Modern Architecture in Britain*, Batsford, London, 1959

DILLISTONE 1929
George Dillistone, *The Planning and Planting of Little Gardens* (with notes and criticisms by Lawrence Weaver), Country Life & George Newnes, London, and Scribner, New York, 1929

DILLISTONE 1930
George Dillistone (ed.), *Dykes on Iris: A Report on the Contribution of the Late W.R. Dykes to Various Journals and Periodicals of the Last Twenty Years of his Life*, Iris Society, Tunbridge Wells, 1930

DRAPER AND EDEN 1970
Marie Draper and W.A. Eden, *Marble Hill House and its Owners*, Greater London Council, London, 1970

ELLIOTT 1986
Brent Elliott, *Victorian Gardens*, Batsford, London, 1986

ELLIOTT 1995
Brent Elliott, *The Country House Garden from the Archives of Country Life 1897–1939*, Mitchell Beazley, London, 1995

GLEW 2001
Adrian Glew (ed.), *Stanley Spencer – Letters and Writings*, Tate Publishing, London, 2001

GOULD 1996
Jeremy Gould, 'Gazetteer of Modern Houses', *Twentieth Century Architecture 2: The Modern House Revisited*, The Journal of the Twentieth Century Society, London, 1996, pp. 111–28

GRAVES AND HODGE 1941
Robert Graves and Alan Hodge, *The Long Weekend: A Social History of Great Britain 1918–1939*, Readers' Union Ltd with Faber and Faber, London, 1941

HARRIS 2010
Alexandra Harris, *Romantic Moderns*, Thames & Hudson, London, 2010

HARVEY AND RETTIG 1985
Sheila Harvey and Stephen Rettig, *Fifty Years of Landscape Design*, The Landscape Press, London, 1985

HARVEY 1998
Sheila Harvey (ed.), *LDT Monographs No. 1: Geoffrey Jellicoe*, Landscape Design Trust, Reigate, 1998

HEINZE-GREENBERG 1999
Ita Heinze-Greenberg, 'Success, House, and Home', in ed. Regina Stephan, *Eric Mendelsohn Architect 1887–1953*, Monacelli Press, New York, 1999, pp. 175–81

HELMREICH 2002
Anne Helmreich, *The English Garden and National Identity: The Competing Styles of Garden Design, 1870–1914*, Cambridge University Press, Cambridge, 2002

HOWARD 1946
Ebenezer Howard, *Garden Cities of To-Morrow*, Faber and Faber, London, 1946

IMBERT 1993
Dorothée Imbert, *The Modernist Garden in France*, Yale University Press, New Haven and London, 1993

JACKSON 1973
Alan A. Jackson, *Semi-Detached London: Suburban Development, Life and Transport, 1900–39*, George Allen & Unwin Ltd, London, 1973

JACQUES 1985
David Jacques, 'Landscape History', in ed. Harvey and Rettig, *Fifty Years of Landscape Design*, The Landscape Press, London, 1985, pp. 27–43

JACQUES AND WOUDSTRA 2009
David Jacques and Jan Woudstra, *Landscape Modernism Renounced: The Career of Christopher Tunnard (1910–1979)*, Routledge, London, 2009

KHOROCHE 2007
Peter Khoroche, *Ivon Hitchens*, Lund Humphries, Aldershot, 2007

LANCASTER 1936
Osbert Lancaster, *Progress at Pelvis Bay*, John Murray, London, 1936

LANCASTER 1938
Osbert Lancaster, *Pillar to Post: English Architecture without Tears*, John Murray, London, 1938

LE CORBUISER 1946
Le Corbusier, *Towards a New Architecture*, Architectural Press, London, 1946

LINDSAY AND WASHINGTON 1952
Donald Lindsay and E.S. Washington, *A Portrait of Britain between the Exhibitions, 1851–1951*, Clarendon Press, Oxford, 1952

LONDON 1999
Charles Mahoney 1903–1968, exh. cat., The Fine Art Society in association with Paul Liss, London, 1999

LONDON, BELFAST AND MANCHESTER 2004
Nicholas Alfrey, Stephen Daniels and Martin Postle (eds.), *Art of the Garden: The Garden in British Art, 1800 to the Present Day*, exh. cat., Tate Britain, London, Ulster Museum, Belfast, and Manchester Art Gallery, 2004

LOUSLEY 1946
J. Edward Lousley, 'Wild Flowers in the City of London', *The Geographical Magazine*, February 1946, p. 413

MAWSON 1994
David Mawson, 'Thomas Mawson at Wood and the Early Twentieth-Century Garden' in ed. Steven Pugsley, *Devon Gardens: An Historical Survey*, Alan Sutton, Stroud, 1994, pp. 106–24

MCCARTHY 1997
Fiona McCarthy, *Stanley Spencer: An English Vision*, Yale University Press, New Haven and London, 1997

MERCER 1937
F.A. Mercer (ed.), *Gardens and Gardening 1937*, The Studio, London, 1937

MUMFORD 1938
Lewis Mumford, *The Culture of Cities*, Secker & Warburg, London, 1938

OLIVER 1981
Paul Oliver, *Dunroamin: The Suburban Semi and its Enemies*, Pimlico, London, 1981

ORWELL 1990
George Orwell, *Coming Up for Air*, Penguin, Harmondsworth, 1990

OSBORN AND WHITTICK 1963
Frederick Osborn and Arnold Whittick, 'The Experimental New Towns', in *The New Towns: The Answer to Megalopolos*, Leonard Hill, London, 1963

OXFORD 1975
Sir John Rothenstein, *Charles Mahoney: A tribute on the occasion of a Memorial Exhibition 1st–25th October 1975, Michael Parkin Gallery, 11 Motcomb Street, London, S.W.1, and 6th November–7th December 1975*, The Ashmolean Museum, Oxford, 1975

POPLE 1991
Kenneth Pople, *Stanley Spencer: A Biography*, Collins, London, 1991

POWERS 1987
Alan Powers, 'Labour of Love', *Country Life*, 30 April 1987, p. 120

POWERS 2001
Alan Powers, *Serge Chermayeff: Designer, Architect, Teacher*, RIBA Publications, London, 2001

POWERS 2005
Alan Powers, *Modern: The Modern Movement in Britain*, Merrell, London and New York, 2005

PRITCHARD 1984
Jack Pritchard, *View from a Long Chair: The Memoirs of Jack Pritchard*, Routledge & Kegan Paul, London, 1984

QUEST-RITSON 2001
Charles Quest-Ritson, *The English Garden: A Social History*, Viking, London, 2001

RAVETZ 1995
Alison Ravetz, 'Gardens and External Space', in *The Place of Home: English Domestic Environments, 1914–2000*, E. & F.N. Spon, London, 1995

RICE AND EVANS 1972
Brian Rice and Tony Evans, *The English Sunrise*, Mathews Miller Dunbar, London, 1972

RICHARDS 1946/1973
J.M. Richards, *The Castles on the Ground*, John Murray, London, 1946/1973

ROTHENSTEIN 1979
John Rothenstein (ed.), *Stanley Spencer, The Man: Correspondences and Reminiscences*, Paul Elek, London, 1979

ROTHENSTEIN 1980
John Rothenstein, *Time's Thievish Progress – Autobiography, Volume III*, Cassell, London, 1980

ROTHENSTEIN 1984
John Rothenstein, *Modern English Painters*, 3 vols., Macdonald, London, 1984

RYAN 1997
Deborah S. Ryan, *The Ideal Home through the 20th Century*, Hazar Publishing, London, 1997

SAINT 1999
Andrew Saint (ed.), *London Suburbs*, Merrell Holberton, London, 1999

SHARP 1936
Thomas Sharp, *English Panorama*, J.M. Dent & Sons, London, 1936

SHARP 1940
Thomas Sharp, *Town Planning*, Penguin, Harmondsworth, 1940

SMILES 1998
Sam Smiles (ed.), *Going Modern and Being British*, Intellect, Exeter, 1998

SOISSONS 1988
Maurice de Soissons, *Welwyn Garden City: A Town Designed for Healthy Living*, Publications for Companies, Cambridge, 1988

SPENCER 1961
Gilbert Spencer, *Stanley Spencer*, Gollancz, London, 1961

SWENARTON 1981
Mark Swenarton, *Homes Fit for Heroes: The Politics and Architecture of Early State Housing in Britain*, Heinemann Educational Books, London, 1981

WAYMARK 2009
Janet Waymark, *Thomas Mawson: Life, Gardens and Landscapes*, Frances Lincoln, London, 2009

WEBBER 1975
Ronald Webber, *Percy Cane Garden Designer*, John Bartholomew & Son, Edinburgh, 1975

WILLIAMS-ELLIS 1928/1996
Clough Williams-Ellis, *England and the Octopus*, Geoffrey Bles, London, 1928; reprinted by CPRE 1996

WILLIAMS-ELLIS 1938
Clough Williams-Ellis, *Britain and the Beast*, J.M. Dent & Sons, London, 1938

YOUNG 1943
G.M. Young (ed.), *Country and Town: A Summary of the Scott and Uthwatt Reports* Penguin, Harmondsworth, 1943

YOUNG 1934
Terence Young, *Becontree and Dagenham: A Report made for the Pilgrim Trust*, Sidders and Son, London, 1934

YOUNGMAN 1985
Peter Youngman, 'Landscape Planning', in ed. Sheila Harvey and Stephen Rettig, *Fifty Years of Landscape Design 1934–84*, The Landscape Press, London, 1985, pp. 45–52

YOUNGMAN 1987
Peter Youngman, 'Peter Youngman', in ed. Sheila Harvey, *Reflections on Landscape: The Lives and Work of Six British Landscape Architects*, Gower Technical Press, London, 1987, pp. 105–37

PHOTOGRAPHIC CREDITS

Aberdeen Art Gallery and Museums Collections / ©The Estate of Stanley Spencer 2011. All rights reserved DACS: fig. 1

Courtesy The Architectural Review: fig. 35

Art Gallery of Ontario, Toronto, Canada /The Bridgeman Art Library. ©The Estate of Stanley Spencer 2011. All rights reserved DACS: fig. 20

Birmingham Museums and Art Gallery / ©The Estate of Stanley Spencer 2011. All rights reserved DACS: figs. 14, 23

Dundee Art Galleries and Museums ©The Estate of Stanley Spencer 2011. All rights reserved DACS: fig. 3

Collection of the Dunedin Public Art Gallery: fig. 17

Courtesy the Estate of Cedric Morris: fig. 25

©The Estate of Stanley Spencer 2011. All rights reserved DACS: fig. 4

Ferens Art Gallery, Hull Museums, UK / ©The Bridgeman Art Library: figs. 7, 9

Ferens Art Gallery: Hull Museums: fig. 13

Courtesy of the Harris Museum & Art Gallery, Preston / ©The Estate of Stanley Spencer 2011. All rights reserved DACS: cover, fig. 21

Heslington, Univeristy of York, Borthwick Institute © 2011

Jane Brown, The English Garden in Our Time, Woodbridge Antique Collector's Club, 1986 © Country Life: fig. 33

Kirklees Collection, Huddersfield Art Gallery ©The Estate of Stanley Spencer 2011. All rights reserved DACS: fig. 2

Laing Art Gallery, Tyne & Wear Archives & Museums ©The Estate of Stanley Spencer 2011. All rights reserved DACS: fig. 5

Leamington Spa Art Gallery and Museum (Warwick District Council): fig. 39

Leeds Museums and Galleries (City Art Gallery) U.K. / The Bridgeman Art Library ©The Estate of Stanley Spencer 2011. All rights reserved DACS: fig. 6

© acknowledged as M.O. Dell & H.L. Wainwright: fig. 34

image © Manchester City Galleries ©The Estate of Stanley Spencer 2011. All rights reserved DACS: fig. 15

Photo © Plymouth City Museum & Art Gallery/ ©The Estate of Stanley Spencer 2011. All rights reserved DACS: fig. 10

Private Collection; by permission ©DACS: fig. 38

Private Collection ©The Estate of Stanley Spencer 2011. All rights reserved DACS: figs. 16, 43

Touchstones - Rochdale Art Gallery: fig. 8

© Royal Academy of Arts, London; Photographer: John Hammond: fig. 18

R.W.A. Permanent Collection: fig. 26

Photo Scala Florence/Heritage Images: fig. 29

Stanley Spencer Gallery Cookham, Barbara Karmel Bequest, ©The Estate of Stanley Spencer 2011. All rights reserved DACS: figs. 11, 37

Stanley Spencer Gallery Cookham, Spencer/Chute correspondence: fig. 12

©Tate, London 2011: fig. 27

©Tullie House Museum and Art Gallery: fig. 22

©The Trustees of the British Museum: fig. 19

Photograph reproduced courtesy the Trustees of National Museums Northern Ireland ©The Estate of Stanley Spencer 2011. All rights reserved DACS: fig. 36

COLOPHON

First pulished on the occasion of the exhibition
Stanley Spencer and the English Garden
at Compton Verney, Warwickshire, 25 June – 2 October 2011

ISBN 978 1 907372 12 4

British Library Cataloguing in Publication Data.
A catalogue record of this book is available from the British Library

Produced by Paul Holberton publishing
89 Borough High Street, London, SE1 1NL
www.paul-holberton.net

Design by Laura Parker

Printed by E-Graphic in Verona, Italy

JACKET: Stanley Spencer, *Wisteria, Cookham*, 1942 (detail of fig. 21)
FRONTISPIECE: Stanley Spencer, *Red Magnolia*, 1938 (detail of fig. 22)
PAGES 6–7: Stanley Spencer, *Cottages at Burghclere*, 1930 (detail of fig. 4)